Close *Reading*

11-14

SUPPORT EDITION

Comprehension, Interpretation and Language Activities

Mary M Firth
Andrew G Ralston

Illustrations by
Miranda Ralston and
Moira Munro

D1332523

Hodder Gibson

A M   **A L I S**

1761298

The Publishers would like to thank the following for permission to reproduce copyright material:

The Kingdom by the Sea © Robert Westall 1990; *Thimble Summer* © Elizabeth Enright 1966; Extracts from *The Cay* by Theodore Taylor, published by The Bodley Head. *Reprinted by permission of the Random House Group Ltd*; *A Dog So Small* © Philippa Pearce, 1962, 1964; *When Hitler Stole Pink Rabbit* © Judith Kerr (1971) Reprinted by permission of HarperCollins Publishers Ltd; *A Series of Unfortunate Events* © Lemony Snicket. Published by Egmont Books Limited, London and used with permission; *Shoes Were for Sunday* © Molly Weir; *On the Island* © Iain Crichton Smith by permission of Birlinn Ltd; Extracts from *Paddy Clark Ha Ha Ha*, published by Secker & Warburg. *Reprinted by permission of The Random House Group Ltd*; *The Wind Singer* © William Nicholson. Published by Egmont Books Limited and used with permission; *Ash Road* by permission of Ivan Southall; *The War of the Worlds* © H G Wells reprinted with the permission of A P Watt Ltd on behalf of The Literary Executors of the Estate of H G Wells; *The Lost Continent* © Bill Bryson. Extracted from *The Lost Continent* by Bill Bryson, published by Black Swan, a division of Transworld Publishers. All rights reserved. *Bee Season* © Myla Goldberg (2000). Reprinted by permission of HarperCollins Publishers Ltd.

Illustrations © Miranda Ralston, pages 6–116.
Illustrations © Moira Munro, pages 2–5.

Photos: Corbis (page 42, Australian Picture Library page 88, Ira Nowinski page 43, James Lauritz page 84, Lester Lefkowitz page 102), Egmont Books Ltd. Page 78, Hulton Archives (Haywood Magee page 52), Popperfoto page 56, Random House page 72, Rex Features (Charles Sykes page 56), Ronald Grant Archives page 91, Team Sputnik for Graphic Classics, 2000 page 95, Alamy (Stephen Saks Photography page 98).

Every effort has been made to trace all copyright holders, but if any have been inadvertently overlooked the Publishers will be pleased to make the necessary arrangements at the first opportunity.

Although every effort has been made to ensure that website addresses are correct at time of going to press, Hodder Gibson cannot be held responsible for the content of any website mentioned in this book. It is sometimes possible to find a relocated web page by typing in the address of the home page for a website in the URL window of your browser.

Papers used in this book are natural, renewable and recyclable products. They are made from wood grown in sustainable forests. The logging and manufacturing processes conform to the environmental regulations of the country of origin.

Orders: please contact Bookpoint Ltd, 130 Milton Park, Abingdon, Oxon OX14 4SB. Telephone: (44) 01235 827720. Fax: (44) 01235 400454. Lines are open from 9.00 – 6.00, Monday to Saturday, with a 24-hour message answering service. Visit our website at www.hoddereducation.co.uk. Hodder Gibson can be contacted direct on: Tel: 0141 848 1609; Fax: 0141 889 6315; email: hoddergibson@hodder.co.uk

© Mary M Firth, Andrew G Ralston 2005
First published in 2005 by
Hodder Gibson, a member of the Hodder Headline Group
2a Christie Street
Paisley PA1 1NB

ISBN-10: 0 340-90610-3
ISBN-13: 978-0-340-90610-1

| Impression number | 10 9 8 7 6 5 4 3 2 1 |
| Year | 2010 2009 2008 2007 2006 2005 |

ISBN-10: 0 340-90611-1
ISBN-13: 978-0-340-90611-8

| Impression number | 10 9 8 7 6 5 4 3 2 1 |
| Year | 2010 2009 2008 2007 2006 2005 |

Typeset in Stone Serif 11 point by Fakenham Photosetting Limited, Fakenham, Norfolk
Printed and bound in Great Britain by Martins the Printers, Berwick-upon-Tweed

A catalogue record for this title is available from the British Library

Contents

Introduction

The fifteen passages in this book are identical to those in *Close Reading 11–14* but the questions and some of the follow-up exercises are different. This 'support' edition has been prepared in response to requests from teachers who wish to use the book in mixed ability classes where some pupils work at a slower pace than others. Because the passages in both are the same, it would be possible to use the two editions in the same classroom.

The layout does not follow the exact format used in national test papers but many of the questions reflect the style used in the Scottish Qualifications Authority's reading tests. In each chapter there are questions which test the following skills:

• Identifying relevant information and main ideas
• Showing understanding of vocabulary
• Showing understanding of the writer's craft

Changes in the questions and exercises compared to the standard edition of *Close Reading* include:

• Definitions of selected words are given
• Some questions have been replaced by simpler ones
• There are more one-mark questions
• More line references are provided to guide pupils towards the location of the required answer
• Follow-up 'For Practice' exercises have been simplified
• Close Reading exercises have all been shortened to 20 marks

MMF/AGR

GETTING STARTED

What is Close Reading?

Close Reading aims to test your understanding of language. You will be given a page or two of a story to read. Your teacher may read it aloud to you, or you may be asked to read it silently.

Then you will be asked questions which will make you think about what you have read. In the questions, the story may be called 'the passage' or 'the text'. Sometimes you will work alone; other times you may discuss the questions with a partner or a group. You will then have to write down answers to the questions.

What a shame!

You should think about what the writer is saying in the story and how you feel about it. The ideas might make you feel angry with someone, for example. Or you might find a story funny or sad.

What are the numbers down the side of the story?

These are line numbers. They are numbered in 5s. They help you find something in the story more easily. For example, if you are asked to look at line 17, you should find line 15 and then count down two more lines. Often a question will direct you to certain lines.

Look at lines 1–14

How does the writer present the situation effectively? . . .

Is there a right way to answer the questions?

Yes. An important rule is to **use your own words** if you are asked to do so. If these words are used in a question, do *not* just copy out part of the text. However, if you are asked to 'find a word in the passage' or if you are asked to 'QUOTE' you may then use words straight from the text.

Do I need to answer in sentences or will one word do?

Sometimes a question will ask you just to pick out a word or expression and a sentence is not required. In other questions you will simply have to tick a box saying 'TRUE' or 'FALSE'. If the question asks you to **explain** something, you should write in sentences. Often, 'bullet point' answers in note form will do. For example, the answer to Question 6 on page 16 could look like this:

Question 6.

• Setting the table
• Fetching milk and butter from the cold room

Will the questions be in any special order?

Usually, the answers will come in the order they are in the story. The first questions will deal with the opening paragraph, and so on. Often you will be directed to certain lines in the story to find the answer.

Why are the numbers of marks given after each question?

This is to help you. If a question is worth just 1 mark, one simple answer is needed. If the question is worth 2 marks, you will need to make two points, or answer in more detail.

What sort of things will the questions ask?

The questions will deal with two main things:

★ What the writer is saying – the **meaning**.

★ How he/she says it – the **style**.

What kind of things will be asked about in style questions?

Style questions deal with *how* a writer tells a story. You will be expected to think about the writer's choice of words and the use of figures of speech such as similes.

Chapter 1

The Kingdom by the Sea

This novel by Robert Westall was published in 1990 but is set in the North of England in the 1940s at the time of the Second World War.

Extract

1   He was an old hand at air raids now.

    As the yell of the siren climbed the sky, he came smoothly out of his dreams. Not scared. Only his stomach clamped down tight for action, as his hands found his clothes laid ready in the dark.

5   Hauled one jumper, then another, over his pyjamas. Thrust both stockinged feet together through his trousers and into his shoes. Then bent to tie his laces thoroughly. A loose lace had tripped him once, in the race to the shelter. He remembered the smashing blow as the ground hit his chin; the painful week after, not able

10   to eat with a bitten tongue.

    He grabbed his school raincoat off the door, pulling the door wide at the same time. All done by feel; no need to put the light on. Lights were dangerous.

15 He passed Dulcie's door, heard Mam and Dulcie muttering to each other, Dulcie sleepy and cross, Mam sharp and urgent. Then he thundered downstairs, the crack of light from the kitchen door lighting up the edge of each stair-tread. Dad was sitting in his warden's uniform, hauling on his big black boots, his grey hair standing up vertically in a bunch.

20 There was a strong smell of Dad's sweaty feet, and the fag he had burning in the ashtray. That was all Harry had time to notice; he had his own job – the two objects laid ready in the chair by the door. The big roll of blankets, wrapped in a groundsheet because the shelter was damp, done up with a big leather strap of 25 Dad's. And Mam's precious attaché case with the flask of hot coffee and insurance policies and other important things, and the little bottle of brandy for emergencies. He heaved the blankets on to his back, picked up the case with one hand and reached to unlock the back door with the other.

30 'Mind that light,' said Dad automatically. But Harry's hand was already reaching for the switch. He'd done it all a hundred times before.

He slammed the door behind him, held his breath and listened. A single aircraft's engines, far out to sea. *Vroomah,* 35 *vroomah, vroomah.* A Jerry. But nothing to worry about yet. Two guns fired, one after another. Two brilliant points of white, lighting up a black landscape of greenhouse, sweet-pea trellises and cucumber-frames. A rolling carpet of echoes. Still out to sea. Safe, then.

40 He ran down the long back garden, with his neck prickling and the blankets bouncing against his back comfortingly. As he passed the greenhouse the rabbits thumped their heels in alarm. There was a nice cold smell of dew and cabbages. Then he was in through the shelter door, shoving the damp mould-stinking 45 curtain aside.

He tossed the things on to Mam's bunk, found the tiny oil-lamp on the back girder, and lit it and watched the flame grow. Then he lit the candle under the pottery milk-cooler that kept the

Extract continued

50 shelter warm. Then he undid the bundle and laid out the blankets on the right bunks and turned back to the shelter door, ready to take Dulcie from Mam. He should be hearing their footsteps any second now, the patter of Mam's shoes and the crunch of Dad's hobnailed boots. Dad always saw them safe in the shelter, before he went on duty. Mam would be nagging Dad – had he locked
55 the back door against burglars? They always teased Mam about that; she must think burglars were bloody brave, burgling in the middle of air raids.

God, Mam and Dad were taking their time tonight. What was keeping them? That Jerry was getting closer. More guns were
60 firing now. The garden, every detail of it, the bird-bath and the concrete rabbit, flashed black, white, black, white, black. There was a whispering in the air. Gun-shrapnel falling like rain . . . they shouldn't be out in *that*. Where were they? Where *were* they? Why weren't they tumbling through the shelter door, panting
65 and laughing to be safe?

That Jerry was right overhead. *Vroomah. Vroomah. Vroomah.*

And then the other whistling. Rising to a scream. Bombs. Harry began to count. If you were still counting at ten, the bombs had missed you.

70 The last thing he remembered was saying 'seven'.

Did you know . . . ?

★ During World War Two, air raid **wardens** (line 18) would patrol the streets and check that no lights were showing in houses. Can you think why this was important?

★ An **attaché case** (line 25) is a briefcase for carrying documents.

★ A **trellis** (line 37) is a framework of criss-cross wooden strips used to support plants.

★ A **girder** (line 47) is a strong metal beam used to support a building.

★ A **milk-cooler** (line 48) was a pottery container which would keep the milk cool. Remember that few people would have fridges at this time.

Questions

Read lines 1–10.

1 What was it that woke Harry up? *(1 mark)*

2 QUOTE the words which tell you how he felt when he woke up. *(1 mark)*

3 Why did he tie his laces 'thoroughly'? *(1 mark)*

Read lines 11–19.

4 'All done by feel' (line 12). Why did Harry not put on the light? *(1 mark)*

5 Who do you think Dulcie was? *(1 mark)*

6 a) QUOTE the word that describes how Harry went down the stairs. *(1 mark)*
   b) What does this word tell us about the manner in which he went downstairs? *(1 mark)*

7 QUOTE the word that suggests his Dad found it quite difficult to pull on his boots. *(1 mark)*

Read lines 20–32.

8 What were the TWO things that Harry had to take with him when he left the house? *(2 marks)*

9 QUOTE the words which show that Harry was very used to these air raids. *(1 mark)*

Read lines 33–45.

10 'Nothing to worry about yet.' Explain why Harry was not worried. *(2 marks)*

Read lines 46–57.

11 Name TWO things that Harry did when he reached the air raid shelter. *(2 marks)*

12 a) Pick out one word from the following list which you think best describes the way he goes about his tasks:

   helpful   well-organised   careless
   thorough   knowledgeable   lazy *(1 mark)*
   b) Explain why you chose this word. *(1 mark)*

Read lines 58–70.

13 a) What do you notice about the punctuation of some of the sentences here? *(1 mark)*
   b) Why do you think the writer has punctuated the sentences in this way? *(1 mark)*

14 What do you think has happened at the end of the story? *(1 mark)*

TOTAL MARKS: 20

Taking a closer look . . .

Similes

When a writer is describing a person or a scene, he often compares it to something we already know so that we can form a clearer picture in our minds.

For example, the passage talks about

> Gun-shrapnel falling like rain.

'Shrapnel' refers to a type of explosive shell which was filled with small pieces of metal. Not many readers will have been exposed to gunfire of this kind, but everyone knows what rain feels like.

An expression which compares one thing to another and uses the word 'like' or 'as' is called a **simile**.

For practice (1)

Each of the following sentences contains a simile.

Decide what is being compared to what in each case.

Explain one way in which the two things are similar, and one way in which they are not.

1. She was running about like a headless chicken.
2. I woke up in the morning feeling as fresh as a daisy.
3. I didn't enjoy the party at all – I felt like a fish out of water.
4. The poet Robert Burns wrote: 'My love is like a red, red rose.'
5. What is it about Steve? He's like a magnet to the girls!

For practice (2)

Many well-known expressions contain similes.

- Fill in the gaps in the following sentences by choosing a word from the list below.
- In groups, discuss what these sayings mean and try to work out how they came about.

1 As bold as _____

2 As cunning as a _____

3 As cool as a _____

4 Last night I slept like a _____

5 He ran like a _____

6 She was as busy as a _____

7 As quick as _____

8 He came down like a ton of _____

9 She was as light as a _____

10 The baby was as quiet as a _____

bee	fox	hare	lightning	log
cucumber	bricks	mouse	feather	brass

Metaphors

Sometimes, instead of suggesting that one thing is *like* another, a writer might make a comparison by saying that one thing *is* another. This kind of comparison is called a **metaphor.**

Here are two examples:

There was a mountain of paperwork waiting for me on my desk.

The pile of papers is compared to a mountain to show how high it was. A metaphor has been used instead of a simile like 'the pile of papers was as high as a mountain'.

In the passage, the distant sound of the German bombers is described as

A rolling carpet of echoes.

Here, the way that the muffled sound of the aircraft reaches the land is compared to a carpet. Why do you think that the writer makes this comparison?

For practice (3)

Each of the following sentences contains a metaphor.

Decide what is being compared to what in each case.

Explain one way in which the two things are similar, and one way in which they are not.

1 At last I've found the key to the whole problem.
2 The fields were covered in a blanket of snow.
3 We tried to find our way but got lost in the maze of streets.
4 The teacher's ice-cold stare made the girl feel very nervous.
5 Education is the gateway to adult life.

For Further Study

More information and exercises on **Similes** and **Metaphors** can be found in *Knowledge About Language*, pages 117–119.

Chapter 2

Thimble Summer

Thimble Summer by Elizabeth Enright is the story of a young girl called Garnet Linden and her brother Jay. They live on a farm in the American Midwest. After there has been no rain for a long time, Garnet's parents are worried that the crops will be ruined. Then one day Garnet finds a silver thimble in the river bank and their luck at once begins to change.

This story was based on the writer's own life on a farm in America.

Extract

1   Garnet thought this must be the hottest day that had ever been in the world. Every day for weeks she had thought the same thing, but this was really the worst of all. This morning the thermometer outside the village drugstore[1] had pointed a thin red
5   finger to one hundred and ten degrees Fahrenheit.

      It was like being inside of a drum. The sky like a bright skin was stretched tight above the valley, and the earth, too, was tight and hard with heat. Later, when it was dark, there would be a noise of thunder, as though a great hand beat upon the drum;
10   there would be heavy clouds above the hills, and flashes of heat lightning, but no rain. It had been like that for a long time. After supper each night her father came out of the house and looked up at the sky, then down at his fields of corn and oats. "No," he would say, shaking his head, "No rain tonight."

15   The oats were turning yellow before their time, and the corn leaves were torn and brittle, rustling like newspaper when the dry wind blew upon them. If the rain didn't come soon there would be no corn to harvest, and they would have to cut the oats for hay. Garnet looked up at the smooth sky angrily, and
20   shook her fist. "You!" she cried, "Why in time can't you let ➤

down a little rain!" At each step her bare feet kicked up a small cloud of dust. There was dust in her hair, and up her nose, making it tickle.

Slowly Garnet walked to the yellow house under tall maple
25 trees and opened the kitchen door. Her mother was cooking supper on the big black coal stove, and her little brother Donald sat on the floor making a noise like a train.

Her mother looked up. Her cheeks were red from the hot stove. "Any mail, darling?" she asked. "Bills," replied Garnet.
30 "Oh," said her mother and turned back to her cooking.

Garnet set the table by the open window. Knife, fork, knife, fork, knife, fork, knife, fork but only a spoon for Donald, who managed even that so absentmindedly that there was usually as much cereal on the outside of him as inside at the end of a meal.
35 Then she went down to the cold room.

It was still and dim down there. A spigot[2] dripped peacefully into the deep pool of water below, where the milk cans and stone butter crock were sunk. Garnet filled a pitcher[3] with milk and put a square of butter on the plate she had brought. She knelt down
40 and plunged both her arms into the water. It was cloudy with spilled milk but icy cold. She could feel coolness spreading through all her veins and a little shiver ran over her.

Going in the kitchen again was like walking into a red-hot oven.

45   Donald had stopped being a train and had become a fire engine. He charged round and round the room hooting and shrieking. How could he be so lively, Garnet wondered. He didn't even notice the awful heat although his hair clung to his head like wet feathers and his cheeks were red as radishes.

50   Her mother looked out of the window. "Father's coming in," she said. "Garnet, don't give him the mail now, I want him to eat a good supper. Put it behind the calendar and I'll tend to it afterwards." Garnet hastily pushed the bills behind the calendar on the shelf over the sink.

55   The screen door opened with its own particular squeak and her father came in. He went to the sink and washed his hands. He looked tired and his neck was sun-burned. "What a day!" he said. "One more like this—" and he shook his head.

It was too hot to eat. Garnet hated her cereal. Donald whined
60   and upset his milk. Jay was the only one who really ate in a business-like manner, as if he enjoyed it. He could probably eat the shingles off a house if there was nothing else handy, Garnet decided.

After she had helped with the dishes, Garnet and Jay put on
65   their bathing suits and went down to the river. They had to go down a road, through a pasture, and across half a dozen sand bars before they came to a place that was deep enough to swim in. This was a dark, quiet pool by a little island; trees hung over it and roots trailed in it. Three turtles slid from a log as the children
70   approached, making three slowly widening circles on the still surface.

"It looks like tea," said Garnet, up to her neck in brownish lukewarm water.

"Feels like it too," said Jay. "I wish it was colder."

75   Still it was water and there was enough of it to swim in. When they were finally sufficiently waterlogged to be red-eyed and streaming, they went exploring on the sandy flats that had emerged from the river during the weeks of drought. They

Extract continued

wandered in different directions, bending over, examining and
80 picking things up. The damp flats had a rich, muddy smell. After
a while the sun set brilliantly behind the trees, but the air seemed
no cooler.

Garnet saw a small object, half-buried in the sand, and
glittering. She knelt down and dug it out with her finger. It was a
85 silver thimble! She dropped the old shoe, bits of polished glass,
and a half dozen clam-shells she had collected and ran
breathlessly to show Jay.

"It's solid silver!" she shouted triumphantly, "and I think it
must be magic too!"

90 "Magic!" said Jay. "Don't be silly, there isn't any such thing."

1 drugstore: shop selling refreshments and other things
2 spigot: a tap
3 pitcher: jug

Questions

1 QUOTE a **phrase** from the first paragraph which tells you
what the weather is like. *(1 mark)*

2 'It was **like** being inside of a drum'. (line 6)
   a) What figure of speech is used in this expression? *(1 mark)*
   b) Write down one other example of this figure of
   speech from the same paragraph (lines 6–14) *(1 mark)*

3 What was unusual about the thunderstorm described in
lines 8–11? *(1 mark)*

4 Read lines 15–23.
Write down ONE phrase which shows the crops are
suffering in the very dry weather. *(1 mark)*

5 Read lines 29–30. ('"Any mail, darling?" … cooking.')
Explain why the mail has made Garnet's mother feel
so depressed. *(1 mark)*

6 Read lines 31–39. ('Garnet set the table … she had
brought'.)
Identify TWO jobs which Garnet does to help her mother
in the house. *(2 marks)*

7   Read again the description of 'the cold room' in
    lines 36–42.
    Pick out ONE word or phrase from this paragraph which
    suggests the cool room was a pleasant place.   *(1 mark)*

8   Read lines 45–49.
    a) QUOTE ONE word from this paragraph which shows
            that Donald was full of energy in spite of the 'awful
            heat' in the kitchen.   *(1 mark)*
    b) Explain **in your own words** one sign that Donald
            was suffering from the heat although he kept running
            and shouting.   *(1 mark)*

9   Read lines 55–58. ('The screen door … shook his head.')
    a) Do you think Garnet's father *was* or *was not* happy? *(1 mark)*
    b) Explain how you can tell from his words, actions or
            appearance.   *(1 mark)*

10 Read lines 64–67. ('After she had helped … swim in.')
    a) Garnet's house was **close to** / **quite far from** the
            river. Choose the phrase you think is correct. *(1 mark)*
    b) Explain your answer to a).   *(1 mark)*

11 Read lines 72–74. ('It looks like tea … it was colder'.)
    Explain ONE way the river water is 'like tea'.   *(1 mark)*

12 Read lines 83–89.
    Explain TWO things which Garnet does which show she
    is very excited about finding the thimble.   *(2 marks)*

13 **a)** Jay was just as excited as Garnet about finding the
            thimble: TRUE or FALSE?   *(1 mark)*
    b) Give a reason for your answer.   *(1 mark)*

TOTAL MARKS: 20

Taking a closer look (1) . . .

Describing words

Adjectives add more information to nouns. Writers add them to
descriptions of things to present a clearer picture; for example, a
<u>thin</u> <u>red</u> finger.

For Practice (1)

Pick out the adjectives which are used to describe the following
things in the story.

1 corn leaves (lines 15–16) _____ _____

2 stove (line 26) _____ _____

3 pool (line 68) _____ _____

4 water in the pool (lines 72–73) _____ _____

5 smell of sand flats (line 80) _____ _____

6 thimble (lines 83–85) _____ _____

Adjectives may also be used to compare things; for example,

fine   finer   finest

These three forms are known as:

positive   comparative   superlative

For Practice (2)

Can you fill in the blanks in this table? The words which have been filled in are all taken from the story.

positive	comparative	superlative
		hottest
		worst
bright		
tall		
lively		
good		
	colder	
	cooler	

Adverbs add more information to verbs. **Adverbs of manner** describe *how* something is done. Most adverbs of manner end in the letters -ly.

For Practice (3)

Fill in the adverb the author of the passage has used in each of the examples below. The line number has been given each time to help you find it. For example:

Garnet looked up at the sky <u>angrily</u>. (line 19)

1 _____ Garnet walked to the yellow house. (line 24)

2 A spigot dripped _____ . (line 36)

3 Garnet _____ pushed the bills behind the calendar. (line 53)

4 The sun set _____ behind the trees. (line 81)

5 Garnet ran _____ to show Jay the thimble. (line 87)

6 "It's solid silver!" she shouted _____. (line 88)

For Further Study

More information and exercises on **Describing Words** can be found in *Knowledge About Language*, pages 26–33

Taking a closer look (2) . . .

Alliteration

Sometimes writers choose words beginning with the same sound to make a phrase stand out. In this story, Garnet's brother Donald's cheeks are described as being '**red as radishes**'. Because the word 'radishes' also begins with 'r' it is more effective than saying 'red as tomatoes', for instance.

This technique is called **alliteration**.

For Practice (4)

Suggest an adjective to go with each of the following words from the story to form phrases with alliteration. For example, 'girlish Garnet'.

_____ Donald		_____ sky	
_____ sand		_____ heat	
_____ brother		_____ glass	

Taking a closer look (3) . . .

Tone

Tone is the name given to the feeling which is expressed by a piece of writing. For example, look at Jay's words:

"Magic!" said Jay. "Don't be silly, there isn't any such thing."

The tone of Jay's words is **scornful**. The word 'silly' shows that he thinks Garnet is childish because she believes in luck. He says 'there isn't any such thing'. The exclamation mark after 'Magic!' shows he is making fun of her idea that the thimble might be magic.

For Practice

Say what feeling you think is suggested in each of these pieces of direct speech from the text. That feeling will be the **tone**.

1   Garnet shook her fist. "You!" she cried, "Why in time can't you let down a little rain!"

2   After supper each night her father came out of the house and looked up at the sky, then down at his fields of corn and oats. "No," he would say, shaking his head, "No rain tonight."

3   "It's solid silver!" she shouted triumphantly, "and I think it must be magic too!"

Chapter 3

The Cay

The Cay by Theodore Taylor takes place during the Second World War. The word 'cay' in the title, which is pronounced 'key', means a small island. The story is about a young American boy, Phillip Enright, who at the start of the war is living with his parents on an island called Curacao, in South America. Curacao is a target for the enemy as it is a centre of the oil industry. This extract shows why Phillip's parents decided life on the island was so dangerous that he should be evacuated by ship to the United States.

The story is being told by Phillip himself.

Extract

1   Like silent, hungry sharks that swim in the darkness of the sea, the German submarines arrived in the middle of the night.

I was asleep on the second floor of our narrow, gabled green house in Willemstad, on the island of Curacao, the largest of
5   the Dutch islands just off the coast of Venezuela. I remember that on that moonless night in February 1942, they attacked the big Lago oil refinery on Aruba, the sister island west of us. Then they blew up six of our small lake tankers, the tubby ones that still bring crude oil from Lake Maracaibo to the
10   refinery. One German sub was even sighted off Willemstad at dawn.

The next morning my father said that the Chinese crews on the lake tankers that shuttled crude oil across the sand bars at Maracaibo had refused to sail without naval escorts. He said the
15   refinery would have to close down within a day, and that meant precious petrol and oil could not go to England, or to General Montgomery in the African desert.

For seven days, not a ship moved by the Queen Emma bridge,

21

and there was gloom over Willemstad. The people had been very
20 proud that the little islands of Aruba and Curacao were now
among the most important islands in the world; that victory or
defeat depended on them. They were angry with the Chinese
crews, and on the third day, my father said that mutiny charges
had been placed against them.

25 "But," he said, "you must understand they are very frightened,
and some of the people who are angry with them would not sail
the little ships either."

He explained to me what it must feel like to ride the cargoes
of crude oil, knowing that a torpedo or shell could turn the whole
30 ship into flames any moment. Even though he wasn't a sailor, he
volunteered to help man the lake tankers.

Soon, of course, we might also run out of fresh water. It rains
very little in the Dutch West Indies unless there is a hurricane,
and water from the few wells has a heavy salt content. The big
35 tankers from the United States or England always carried fresh
water to us in ballast, and then it was distilled again so that we
could drink it. But now all the big tankers were being held up in
their ports until the submarines could be chased away.

Towards the end of the week, we began to run out of fresh
40 vegetables because the schooner-men were also afraid. Now, my
mother talked constantly about the submarines, the lack of water,
and the shortage of food. It almost seemed that she was using the
war as an excuse to leave Curacao.

"The ships will be moving again soon," my father said
45 confidently, and he was right.

I think it was February 21 that some of the Chinese sailors
agreed to sail to Lake Maracaibo. But on that same day a
Norwegian tanker, headed for Willemstad, was torpedoed off
Curacao, and fear again swept over the old city. Without our
50 ships we were helpless.

A day or two later, my father took me into the Schottegat[1]
where they were completing the loading of the *SS Empire Tern*, a
big British tanker. She had machine guns fore and aft, one of the
few armed ships in the harbour.

55   Although the trade wind was blowing, the smell of petrol and oil lay heavy over the Schottegat. Other empty tankers were there, high out of the water, awaiting orders to sail once they had cargoes. The men on them were leaning over the rail watching all the activity on the *Empire Tern*. I looked on as the thick hoses that

60   were attached to her quivered when the petrol was pumped into her tanks. The fumes shimmered in the air, and one by one, they "topped" her tanks, loading them right to the brim and securing them for sea. No one said very much. With all that aviation fuel around, it was dangerous.

65   Then in the afternoon, we stood near the pontoon bridge as she steamed slowly down St Anna Bay. Many others had come to watch, too, even the governor, and we all cheered as she passed, setting out on her lonely voyage to England. There, she would help refuel the Royal Air Force.

70   The sailors on the *Empire Tern*, which was painted a dull white but had rust streaks all over her, waved back at us and held up their fingers in a V-for-victory sign.

       We watched until the pilot boat, having picked up the harbour pilot from the *Empire Tern*, began to race back to

75   Willemstad. Just as we were ready to go, there was an explosion, and we looked toward the sea. The *Empire Tern* had vanished in a wall of red flames, and black smoke was beginning to boil into the sky.

       Someone screamed, "There it is." We looked off to one side of

80   the flames, about a mile away, and saw a black shape in the water, very low. It was a German submarine, surfaced now to watch the ship die.

       A tug and several small motorboats headed out toward the *Tern*, but it was useless. Some of the women cried at the sight of

85   her, and I saw men, my father included, with tears in their eyes. It didn't seem possible that only a few hours before I had been standing on her deck. I was no longer excited about the war; I had begun to understand that it meant death and destruction.

¹ Schottegat: harbour at Curacao

Extract continued

Questions

1 Read lines 1–2.
What time of day did the German submarines arrive at
the island of Curacao? *(1 mark)*

2 a) What figure of speech is used in the phrase 'like silent,
hungry sharks'? (line 1) *(1 mark)*
b) Suggest ONE way in which sharks and submarines
are alike and ONE way in which they are *not* alike. *(2 marks)*

3 Read lines 3–11. ('I was asleep … at dawn'.)
Identify ONE piece of damage done by the Germans. *(1 mark)*

4 Read lines 12–31 about the strike of the Chinese sailors.
The answer to each of the following questions is TRUE
or FALSE.
a) The strike of the Chinese sailors lasted a week.
TRUE / FALSE
b) The people on the islands agreed with the sailors'
action. TRUE / FALSE
c) Phillip's father thought the Chinese sailors had good
reason for their action. TRUE / FALSE *(3 marks)*

5 Read lines 40–44. ('Soon, of course … to leave Curacao'.)

Name TWO things the island people were running out of because the ships could not sail. *(2 marks)*

6 Read lines 52–65. ('A day or two … it was dangerous'.)
   a) What kind of ship was the *Empire Tern*? *(1 mark)*
   b) Why do you think loading the *Empire Tern* was so dangerous? *(1 mark)*

7 Read lines 66–73. ('Then in the afternoon … victory sign'.)
   Explain ONE way in which the island people tried to cheer up the crew of the *Empire Tern* as they set out to sea. *(1 mark)*

8 Read lines 74–83. ('We watched … the ship die.')
   Explain what had happened to the *Empire Tern*. *(1 mark)*

9 a) Suggest another word or phrase the writer could have used instead of 'die' in line 83. *(1 mark)*
   b) Explain why the word 'die' was a good choice here. *(1 mark)*

10 Read lines 84–end.
   Tick the box which you think is appropriate:

		True	False
(i)	The small boats were able to help the crew of the *Empire Tern*.	❏	❏
(ii)	Phillip no longer found the idea of war exciting.	❏	❏
(iii)	All the adults were in tears.	❏	❏
(iv)	Phillip had learned something about war from seeing the *Empire Tern* being sunk.	❏	❏

(4 marks)

TOTAL MARKS: 20

Taking a closer look (1) . . .

Nouns

Nouns are naming words. They can be names of things, people, places or ideas.

Words like bag, man, school, James and brightness are all nouns.

For Practice (1)

Read the following paragraph. Then say whether each of the underlined words from it in the following table is a noun or not.

> After the *Empire Tern* was sunk, Phillip's <u>mother</u> decided to <u>send</u> him to <u>America</u>, for his safety. However, the ship <u>he</u> was on was also hit by a torpedo and sunk. Phillip became blind <u>after</u> he was hit on the head. An old black man called Timothy pulled Phillip on to a <u>raft</u> and they floated on it for several days. There was a <u>cat</u> on board also. The three of them arrived at a <u>tiny</u> island. They survived by eating <u>fish</u> and plants. There was a terrible storm and <u>Timothy</u> died trying to protect Phillip. Phillip was rescued after writing 'HELP' on the sand in huge letters. This was noticed by the pilot of an aeroplane who picked him up and took him home. <u>Eventually</u> Phillip got his <u>sight</u> back.

Put a tick or a cross in the correct column for each word. Three are done for you.

Word	Yes	No
mother	✓	
send		
America		
he		
after		✗
raft		
cat		
tiny		
fish	✓	
Timothy		
eventually		
sight		

Common nouns are general names of things. For example, ship.

Proper nouns are names of particular things or people. For example, Phillip.

Abstract nouns are terms expressing ideas or feelings. For example, fear.

Collective nouns are names by which groups of things are known. For example, army.

For Practice (2)

Draw a table with four columns, headed like this:

common	proper	abstract	collective

Then enter each of the following twelve nouns into the column of its type.

shark	darkness	house
Aruba	crew	Montgomery
boat	pilot	water
submarine	victory	destruction

When is a noun not a noun?

Some words can be used as nouns and also as other parts of speech such as verbs or adjectives. For example, 'rain' can be used as a noun: 'the rain was heavy' or as a verb (doing word): 'it began to rain.' (Verbs are explained in Chapter 4.)

For Practice (3)

Do this exercise in pairs.

In the following sentences the underlined words, which are verbs, can also be used as nouns. For each example, compose a sentence of your own in which the underlined word is used as a noun.

Then exchange your sentences with a partner and discuss how many you have got right.

1   The Chinese crews refused to <u>sail</u> without escorts.

2   Phillip's father volunteered to help <u>man</u> the lake tankers.

3   Phillip's mother was using the war as an excuse to <u>leave</u> Curacao.

4   Many others had come to <u>watch</u>, too.

5   The pilot boat began to <u>race</u> back to Willemstadt.

For Further Study

More information and exercises on **Nouns** can be found in *Knowledge About Language*, pages 7–13

Chapter 4

A Dog so Small

Just about every girl and boy goes through the phase of wanting a dog! In her novel **A Dog so Small**, Phillipa Pearce tells the story of a boy called Ben who is so disappointed when he doesn't receive a dog for his birthday. All he gets is a picture of one. At the time he has no idea what strange adventures this picture will lead to. . .

Extract

1   The post had come, and it was all for Ben. His father had piled it by his place for breakfast. There were also presents from May and Dilys, Paul and Frankie; and his mother and father had given him a sweater of the kind deep-sea fishermen wear (from his mother,
5   really) and a Sheffield steel jack-knife (from his father). They all watched while, politely, he opened their presents first of all, and thanked them.

He was not worrying that there had been no dog standing by his place at the breakfast-table. He was not so green as to think
10 that postmen delivered dogs.

But there would be a letter – from his grandfather, he supposed – saying when the dog would be brought, by a proper carrier, or where it could be collected from. Ben turned eagerly from his family's presents to his post.

15 He turned over the letters first, looking for his grandfather's handwriting; but there was nothing. Then he looked at the writing on the two picture-postcards that had come for him – although you would hardly expect anything so important to be left to a postcard. There was nothing. Then he began to have the
20 feeling that something might have gone wrong after all. He remembered, almost against his will, that his grandfather's promise had been only a whisper and a nod, and that not all promises are kept, anyway.

He turned to the parcels, and at once saw his grandfather's
25 handwriting on a small flat one. Then he knew for certain that
something was wrong. They would hardly send him an ordinary
birthday present as well as one so special as a dog. There was only
one explanation: they were sending him an ordinary present
instead of the dog.
30 'Open it, Ben,' said his mother; and his father reminded him,
'Use your new knife on the string, boy.' Ben never noticed the
sharpness of the Sheffield steel as he cut the string round the
parcel and then unfolded the wrapping paper.
They had sent him a picture instead of a dog.
35

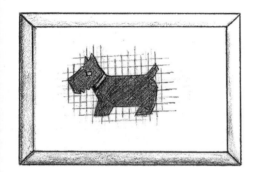

And then he realised that
they had sent him a dog,
after all. He almost hated
them for it. His dog was
worked in woollen cross-
40 stitch, and framed, and
glazed as a little picture.
There was a letter which
explained: 'Dear Ben, Your
grandpa and I send you hearty good wishes for your birthday. We
45 know you would like a dog, so here is one ...'
There was more in the letter, but, with a sweep of his hand, Ben
pushed aside letter, packing-paper, string, and picture. They fell to
the floor, the picture with a sharp sound of breakage. His mother
picked it up. 'You've cracked the glass, Ben, and it's a nice little
50 picture – a little old picture that I remember well.'
'I think it's a funny birthday present for Ben, don't you, Paul?'
said Frankie; and Paul agreed. May and Dilys both thought it was
rather pretty. Mr Blewitt glanced at it and then back to the
newspaper he had opened.
55 Ben said nothing, because he could not. His mother looked at
him, and he knew that she knew that, if he hadn't been so old,
and a boy, he would be crying. 'Your granny treasured this
because it was a present from your Uncle Willy,' said Mrs Blewitt.
'He brought it home as a curio, from his last voyage – the last

Extract continued

60 voyage before he was drowned. So you see, Granny's given you
something that was precious to her.'

But what was dead Uncle Willy or a woolwork dog to Ben? He
still could not trust himself to speak; and now they were all
looking at him, wondering at the silence. Even his father had put
65 the paper down.

'Did you expect a real dog?' Frankie asked suddenly.

Everyone else answered for Ben, anyway.

His mother said, 'Of course not. Ben knows perfectly well that
Granny and Grandpa could never afford to buy him a real dog.'
70 His father said, 'And, anyway, you can't expect to keep a dog
in London nowadays – the traffic's too dangerous.' Ben
remembered the cat scuttering from under the wheels of the car
that morning, and he hated his father for being in the right. 'It
isn't as if we had any garden to let a dog loose in,' went on Mr
75 Blewitt; 'and we're not even near an open space where you could
exercise it properly.'

Questions

Read lines 1–23.

1 Why do you think the writer says that Ben's father 'piled'
the mail beside his place at the breakfast table (line 1),
rather than saying 'placed' or 'put'?   *(1 mark)*

2 What had Ben expected the postman to bring him on
his birthday?   *(1 mark)*

3 Re-read lines 19 to 23.
Give one reason why Ben should not have been so
confident that he would receive the present he wanted.   *(1 mark)*

Read lines 24–61.

4 a) Which of these words best describes how Ben felt
when he saw what his grandparents' gift was?
bored   surprised   angry   *(1 mark)*

b) Which of his actions shows how he felt at this time?   *(1 mark)*

5 Read lines 57–61.
Explain one reason why Ben's mother thought he should
have been more grateful for his grandmother's gift.   *(1 mark)*

Read lines 62–76.

6 Write down TWO reasons why Ben's father, Mr Blewitt,
thought it was not practical for him to have a dog.   *(2 marks)*

7 Think again about the whole passage.
We learn something about Ben's character in this passage.
Write down one feature of his personality and explain
how you worked this out. Lay out your answer like this:
Feature _____   *(1 mark)*
Explanation _____   *(1 mark)*

8 Find ONE word in the passage that means the same as
each of these explanations. State which part of speech
(noun, verb, adjective or adverb) the word is.   *(6 marks)*

MEANING	WORD	PART OF SPEECH
Keen to do something	_____	_____
An article valued because it is unusual or rare	_____	_____
A long journey, usually on board a ship	_____	_____

9 Look at these sentences about the passage. Decide
whether each sentence is **true** or **false** or whether you
can't tell from the passage. Tick **one** box beside
each sentence.   *(4 marks)*

	True	False	Can't Tell
a) Ben's grandfather made a firm promise to get him a dog for his birthday.	☐	☐	☐
b) Ben would have preferred to receive nothing at all from his grandparents rather than the picture they sent.	☐	☐	☐
c) Ben's father did not like dogs.	☐	☐	☐
d) Ben was too upset to make any comment when he opened his gifts.	☐	☐	☐

TOTAL MARKS: 20

Taking a Closer Look . . .

Verbs

A verb is a doing word. It refers to an action, such as eat, drink, walk, sit, jump.

To find the verb in a sentence, ask yourself: what did the person who is the subject of the sentence *do?*

For example, look at this sentence from the passage:

> They all watched while Ben opened their presents.

What did *they* do?
What did *Ben* do?

'Watched' and 'opened' are the verbs.

Four things to remember about verbs

1 A verb is a 'doing' word.

For practice

a) Pick out the verb (doing word) from each of the following sentences:

1 Ben expected a real dog.

2 Ben pushed aside letter, packing-paper, string and picture.

3 Mr Blewitt glanced at the present.

33

4   Uncle Willy brought the picture home from his last voyage.

5   Ben said nothing.

b)   From the list below, choose a suitable verb to fill each gap.

1   The shop _____ all the CDs in the charts.

2   Over the holidays I _____ one of the 'Harry Potter' books.

3   The postman _____ the birthday cards through the letter box.

4   Tracy _____ the most fashionable pair of jeans in the sale.

5   Kathleen _____ the shelving unit by herself.

   read   *picked*   *assembled*   *pushed*   *sold*

---

2   Words like 'be' and 'have' are also verbs.

These can take a number of different forms:

To **be**:	I **am**	To **have**:	I **have**
	you/they **are**		he/she **has**
	he/she/it **is**		I/he/they **had**
	I **was**		
	you/we/they **were**		

For Practice

Pick out or underline the verbs in the following sentences. They are all parts of 'to be' or 'to have'. You will find all of them in the lists above.

1   He is a nice man.

2   My sister has a black cat.

3   We were on holiday last month.

4   You are on the list.

5   I am tired.

6   John had a new bag.

7   I was new at the school last year.

8   We have a black uniform.

9   My mother is a nurse.

10   You have a new hairstyle.

---

3   A verb can be made up of more than a single word.

The plane will be landing at about six o'clock.

Is the verb in this sentence *will?*
Or is it *be?*
Or *landing?*

Remember that the verb describes the **action** taken. The action here is that the plane *will be landing*. These three words are therefore the verb in this sentence.

For practice

a) Underline or write down the verbs in the following sentences. Each verb consists of **two** or **three** words. The first example is done for you.

1 I <u>am going</u> to the party.

2 The team has been trying hard.

3 You have seen that film four times.

4 I will be on holiday next week.

5 Partick Thistle had beaten Rangers.

b) From the list below, choose a suitable verb phrase to fill the gap.

1 We _____ to America next summer, but my parents have not made up their minds yet.

2 Barry _____ by John.

3 I _____ home soon.

4 The detectives _____ for the bank robber.

5 My sister _____ since 8 o'clock this morning.

> *has been working   will be going   was being bullied*
> *are looking   might be going*

---

4 Verbs can be in different tenses.

The job that extra words like 'have been' and 'will be' do in the sentence is to tell you **when** the action takes place. This is called the **tense** of the verb.

Present: I am playing; I play
Future: I will play
Past: I did play; I played; I have played

For practice

a) In the next exercise you must decide whether the action is happening *now* (**present**), whether it is *going to happen in the future* (**future**) or whether it *has already happened* (**past**). Tick the box which you think is the right one. The verbs are underlined to help you.

	Past	Present	Future
a) Ben's birthday <u>will be</u> on Saturday.	❒	❒	❒
b) Ben <u>hated</u> the picture.	❒	❒	❒
c) My dad <u>paints</u> houses.	❒	❒	❒
d) I <u>shall see</u> Jane tomorrow.	❒	❒	❒
e) A dog <u>ran</u> into the playground.	❒	❒	❒

b) (i) Pick out or underline the **ten** verbs in the **present tense** in the following passage.

I wake up in a hot, dry wilderness. I remember that we desperately need water. I sit up and rub my grimy face with my hands and it feels like my eyelids and lips are stuck together. It is not far from dawn but there is none of the bright feel of sunrise in the air. The others are still fast asleep.

(ii) Then rewrite the passage, changing all these verbs from the present tense to the **past tense**.

For Further Study

More information and exercises on **Verbs** can be found in *Knowledge About Language*, pages 13–26

Chapter 5

When Hitler Stole Pink Rabbit

The author, Judith Kerr, based the events in this book on her own early life. The year is 1933, and Hitler has come to power in Germany. Anna, aged 9, and her brother Max, 12, are German Jews. The family has moved to Switzerland to escape the Nazis. However, the Swiss authorities are afraid of offending the Nazis and they will not allow Anna's father, a writer, to work in Switzerland. Anna's parents then think of moving to France so that her father can go on earning a living. They leave Anna and Max with Mr and Mrs Zwirn, a kind Swiss couple who keep an inn. The Zwirns have two children of their own, Vreneli and Franz.

Extract

1   At the end of the second week after Mama and Papa's departure Anna's class went on an excursion into the mountains. They did not get back to the inn until evening. Then, although it was only seven o'clock, she went to bed. On her way upstairs she came
5   upon Franz and Vreneli whispering together in the corridor. When they saw her they stopped.

'What were you saying?' said Anna. She had caught her father's name and something about the Nazis.

'Pa said we weren't to tell you,' said Vreneli unhappily.

10 'For fear of upsetting you,' said Franz. 'But it was in the paper. The Nazis are putting a price on your Pa's head.'

'A price on his head?' asked Anna stupidly.

'Yes,' said Franz. 'A thousand German Marks. Pa says it shows how important your Pa must be. There was a picture of him and all.'

15 How could you put a thousand Marks on a person's head? It was silly. She determined to ask Max when he came up to bed but fell asleep long before.

In the middle of the night Anna woke up. It was quite sudden, like something being switched on inside her head, and she was 20 immediately wide awake. And as though she had been thinking of nothing else all night, she suddenly knew with terrible clarity how you put a thousand Marks on a person's head.

In her mind she saw a room. It was a funny looking room because it was in France and the ceiling, instead of being solid, 25 was a mass of criss-crossing beams. In the gaps between them something was moving. It was dark, but now the door opened and the light came on. Papa was coming to bed. He took a few steps towards the middle of the room. 'Don't!' Anna wanted to cry and then the terrible shower of heavy coins began. It came 30 pouring down from the ceiling on to Papa's head. She called out but the coins kept coming. He sank to his knees under their weight and the coins kept falling and falling until he was completely buried under them.

So this was what Herr[1] Zwirn had not wanted her to know.
This was what the Nazis were going to do to Papa. Or perhaps,
since it was in the paper, they had already done it. She lay staring
into the darkness, sick with fear. In the other bed she could hear
Max breathing quietly and regularly. Should she wake him? But
Max hated being disturbed in the night – he would probably only
be cross and say that it was all nonsense. And perhaps it was all
nonsense, she thought with a sudden lightening of her misery.
Perhaps in the morning she would be able to see it as one of
those silly night fears which had frightened her when she was
younger like the times when she had thought that the house was
on fire, or that her heart had stopped. In the morning there
would be the usual postcard from Mama and Papa and everything
would be all right. Yes, but this was not something she had
imagined – it had been in the paper . . . Her thoughts went round
and round.

But at breakfast there was no postcard from Mama and
Papa.

'Why do you think it hasn't come?' she asked Max.

'Postal delay,' said Max indistinctly through a mouthful of
bread. 'Bye!' and he rushed to catch his train.

'I dare say it'll come this afternoon,' said Herr Zwirn.

There was still no postcard when she came home from school,
nor was there anything in the last post at seven o'clock. It was
the first time that Mama and Papa had not written. Anna
managed to get through supper thinking cool thoughts about
postal delays, but once she was in bed with the light out all the
terror of the previous night came flooding back with such force
that she felt almost choked by it. She tried to remember that she
was a Jew and must not be frightened, otherwise the Nazis would
say that all Jews were cowards – but it was no use. She kept seeing
the room with the strange ceiling and the terrible rain of coins
coming down on Papa's head. Even though she shut her eyes and
buried her face in the pillow she could still see it.

She must have been making some noise in bed for Max
suddenly said, 'What's the matter?'

Extract continued

70   'Oh, you idiot!' he said when she had explained her fears. 'Don't you know what is meant by a price on someone's head? It means offering a reward to anyone who captures that person.'

'There you are!' wailed Anna. 'The Nazis are trying to get Papa!'

75   'Well, in a way,' said Max. 'But Herr¹ Zwirn doesn't think it's very serious – after all there's not much they can do about it as Papa isn't in Germany.'

'You think he's all right?'

'Of course he's all right. We'll have a postcard in the morning.'

80   In the morning instead of a postcard they had a long letter. Mama and Papa had decided that they should all live in Paris together and Papa was coming to collect them.

. . . . . .

'Papa,' said Anna after the first excitement of seeing him safe and
85   sound had worn off. 'Papa, I was a bit upset when I heard about the price on you head.'

'So was I!' said Papa. 'Very upset.'

'Were you?' asked Anna, surprised. Papa had always seemed so brave.

90   'Well, it's such a very small price,' explained Papa. 'A thousand Marks goes nowhere these days. I think I'm worth a lot more, don't you?'

'Yes,' said Anna, feeling better.

'No self-respecting kidnapper would touch it,' said Papa. He
95   shook his head sadly. 'I've a good mind to write to Hitler and complain.'

¹ Herr: Mr

Questions

1 Read lines 1–6.
   Why do you think Franz and Vreneli stopped
   whispering as soon as Anna came upstairs?   *(1 mark)*

2 Read lines 7–14.
Why had Franz and Vreneli's father told them not to tell
Anna what was in the paper? *(1 mark)*

3 'The Nazis are putting a price on your Pa's head.' (line 11)
   a) Who does Anna decide to ask to explain this to her? *(1 mark)*
   b) Why does she not do so? *(1 mark)*

4 Read lines 18–22. ('In the middle … on a person's head'.)
Say whether each of the following is TRUE or FALSE:
   a) Anna woke up slowly. TRUE/FALSE
   b) Anna thought she now understood what the
      sentence meant. TRUE/FALSE *(2 marks)*

5 What figure of speech does the writer use in the
expression 'like something being switched on inside her
head' (line 19)? *(1 mark)*

6 Read lines 23–33. ('In her mind … under them.')
Anna imagines a scene in a room.
   a) Who came into the room? *(1 mark)*
   b) What happened to him in the room? *(2 marks)*

7 **a)** Read lines 34–49.
      QUOTE an expression from lines 34–38 that tells us
      how Anna feels as she lies in the darkness. *(1 mark)*
   b) Give ONE reason from lines 40–49 why she thinks
      she will feel better in the morning. *(1 mark)*

8 Read lines 50–58. ('but at breakfast … had not written.')
Why is Anna still upset in the morning? *(1 mark)*

9 Read lines 58–62. ('Anna managed … almost choked
by it.')
Look at the author's word choice in this sentence. Pick
out TWO words or phrases which express Anna's
extreme fear. *(2 marks)*

10 In lines 71–72 Max explains what 'to have a price on
your head' really means. What is the real explanation? *(1 mark)*

11 Read lines 80–82. ('In the morning … collect them.')
What news do Anna and Max get in the morning? *(1 mark)*

12 When Anna's father returns, Anna says to him, 'I was *a
bit* upset' (line 85). She does not say, 'I was *very* upset'.
Which ONE of the following is *not* a likely reason for this?
   a) She does not want to worry her father.

b) She had not actually been very worried.

c) She does not want to seem foolish or weak.

d) Her fear now seems less disturbing since her father is safe. *(1 mark)*

Read lines 90–92.

13 a) What does Anna's father say he might do about having 'a price on his head'? *(1 mark)*

b) Pick out ONE word which describes his TONE:

    angry   humorous   frightened *(1 mark)*

TOTAL MARKS: 20

Taking a closer look (1) . . .

Point of View

Judith Kerr, the author of *When Hitler Stole Pink Rabbit*, based Anna's adventures on her own early life, when her family, who were also Jews, had to leave Nazi Europe.

In the story, Judith Kerr writes in **the third person**. She talks of 'Anna', 'she' and 'her' and not 'I', 'me' or 'my' when she is presenting Anna's story. However, the story is told from Anna's **point of view**. Anna is the main character in the story. The reader learns about Anna's thoughts and feelings. The reader never knows any more about what is happening than Anna herself does.

Judith Kerr could have written the story in **the first person**, using 'I', 'we', 'me' and 'my', instead of 'Anna', 'they', 'she' and 'her'.

For practice

Look at the opening of the story again:

At the end of the second week after Mama and Papa's departure Anna's class went on an excursion into the mountains. They did not get back to the inn until evening. Then, although it was only seven o'clock, she went to bed. On her way upstairs she came upon Franz and Vreneli whispering together in the corridor. When they saw her they stopped.

'What were you saying?' said Anna. She had caught her father's name .

Rewrite it, as if you *are* Anna, changing from *third* to *first* person. The first two sentences are done for you to start you off.

At the end of the second week after Mama's and Papa's departure, my class went on an excursion into the mountains. We did not get back to the inn until evening. Then, . . .

Taking a closer look (2) . . .

Symbolism

Symbolism is when one thing represents or stands for another. The title of the novel, *When Hitler Stole Pink Rabbit*, can also be seen as symbolic. The title suggests or 'symbolises' something about the treatment of Jewish children under the evil Nazi regime.

When Anna's family leave Berlin, they have to leave almost all of their belongings behind, including Anna's favourite toy, 'Pink Rabbit'. Anna imagines Hitler will take possession of her beloved rabbit.

This is the source of the title of the book. It is comical, since we imagine Adolf Hitler in his Nazi uniform carrying off a child's pink toy rabbit.

However, this may **symbolise** the cruel way in which the Nazis often treated children in real life. Not only did they take their possessions, but also their freedom and in many cases their lives. Have you heard of Anne Frank, the girl who spent two years in hiding only to die in a concentration camp? Many Jewish children under Hitler's regime lost their childhoods. Anna is portrayed as one of the lucky ones who survived.

'A price on his head'.

Look again at Anna's vision (lines 23–33) which you were asked about in questions 5 and 9 after the passage. Discuss the following questions in your groups.

a) What happened in the vision? What did Anna think actually happened to her father?

b) Max explains to Anna the real meaning of the phrase 'to have a price on your head'. What do you think would have happened to Anna's father if someone had turned him in to the Nazis for the reward?

c) Compare your answers to a) and b). How might Anna's vision be seen as symbolic of what might have happened to her father?

Chapter 6

A Series of Unfortunate Events

A Series of Unfortunate Events by Lemony Snicket sold over a million copies in the UK in 2002. There are now ten books in the series, telling the story of the problems faced by the three Baudelaire orphans – Violet, Klaus and Sunny. This extract comes from the first book, 'The Bad Beginning', and describes the three children's experience of meeting their unpleasant relative, Count Olaf.

Extract

1   I don't know if you've ever noticed this, but first impressions are often entirely wrong. You can look at a painting for the first time, for example, and not like it at all, but after looking at it a little longer you may find it very pleasing. The first time you try

5   Gorgonzola cheese you may find it too strong, but when you are older you may want to eat nothing but Gorgonzola cheese. Klaus, when Sunny was born, did not like her at all, but by the time she was six weeks old the two of them were as thick as thieves. Your initial opinion on just about everything may change over time.

10   I wish I could tell you that the Baudelaires' first impressions of Count Olaf and his house were incorrect, as first impressions so often are. But these impressions – that Count Olaf was a horrible person, and his house a depressing pigsty – were absolutely correct. During the first few days after the orphans'

15 arrival at Count Olaf's, Violet, Klaus and Sunny attempted to

20 make themselves feel at home,

Orphans,
To Do:—
Repair Windows
Repaint Porch

46

but it was really no use. Even though Count Olaf's house was quite large, the three children were placed together in one filthy

25

bedroom that had only one small bed in it. Violet and Klaus took turns sleeping in it, so that every other night one of them was in the bed and the other was sleeping on the hard wooden floor, and

30 the bed's mattress was so lumpy it was difficult to say who was more uncomfortable. To make a bed for Sunny, Violet removed the dusty curtains from the curtain rod that hung over the bedroom's one window and bunched them together to form a sort of cushion, just big enough for her sister. However, without

35 curtains over the cracked glass, the sun streamed through the window every morning, so the children woke up early and sore each day. Instead of a closet, there was a large cardboard box that had once held a refrigerator and would now hold the three children's clothes, all piled in a heap. Instead of toys, books, or

40 other things to amuse the youngsters, Count Olaf had provided a small pile of rocks. And the only decoration on the peeling walls was a large and ugly painting of an eye, matching the one on Count Olaf's ankle and all over the house.

But the children knew, as I'm sure you know, that the worst
45 surroundings in the world can be tolerated if the people in them are interesting and kind. Count Olaf was neither interesting nor kind; he was demanding, short-tempered and bad-smelling. The only good thing to be said for Count Olaf is that he wasn't around very often. When the children woke up and chose their

50 clothing out of the refrigerator box, they would walk into the kitchen and find a list of instructions left for them by Count Olaf, who would often not appear until nighttime. Most of the day he spent out of the house, or up in the high tower, where the children were forbidden to go. The instructions he left for them

55 were usually difficult chores, such as repainting the back porch or repairing the windows, and instead of a signature Count Olaf would draw an eye at the bottom of the note. ❑

Questions

Read lines 1–9.

1 From the first paragraph, find another expression which means the same as 'initial opinion'. *(1 mark)*

2 a) In lines 6–8, the writer says that Klaus and his little sister were 'as thick as thieves'. Does this mean:
they were very close to each other and got on well
OR
they weren't very clever
OR
they used to steal things? *(1 mark)*

b) What is the name for an expression like 'as thick as thieves'? *(1 mark)*

Read lines 10–31.

3 QUOTE the words which describe the Baudelaire children's first impressions of (a) Count Olaf and (b) his house. *(2 marks)*

4 In your own words, explain what Violet, Klaus and Sunny tried to do during their first few days at Count Olaf's house. Base your answer on lines 17–22. *(1 mark)*

5 Write down TWO things mentioned in lines 22–31 that the children did not like about the bedroom. *(2 marks)*

Read lines 31–43.

6 a) What did Violet try to do to make Sunny more comfortable? *(2 marks)*

b) What does this tell you about Violet? *(1 mark)*

7 Why do you think there was a picture of an eye painted on the wall and in other places in the house? *(1 mark)*

Read lines 44–57.

8 The word 'tolerated' (line 45) means:
a) enjoyed
b) put up with
c) changed *(1 mark)*

9 In your own words, write down one thing about Count Olaf that the children disliked. *(1 mark)*

10 Where did Count Olaf spend his days? *(1 mark)*

11 Name TWO of the tasks he expected the children to work on. *(2 marks)*

12 How suitable do you think these tasks are for children? Give a reason for your answer. *(2 marks)*

13 Write a sentence giving your opinion of Count Olaf. *(1 mark)*

TOTAL MARKS: 20

Taking a closer look . . .

Writing in sentences (1)

What is it that makes a group of words a sentence?

★ it is a complete statement that makes sense standing on its own
★ it begins with a capital letter and ends with a full stop
★ it contains a verb (a doing word)

For practice (1)

Imagine that a group of words was written on each of the rocks that Count Olaf left the children to play with. Sort out which ones are complete sentences and which ones are not. How can you tell?

1 Count Olaf's house was quite large.
2 Violet and Klaus took turns sleeping on the bed.
3 Instead of toys, books or other things.
4 The sun streamed through the window.
5 Violet removed the curtains.
6 If the people are interesting and kind.
7 Your initial opinion on just about anything.
8 The house was a depressing pigsty.
9 Without curtains over the cracked glass.
10 All over the house.

Creating more complex sentences

A story would make very dull reading if all the sentences were short and simple. Writers usually join short statements into longer ones. There are many ways of doing this, but one of the most useful ways is to use conjunctions (joining words).

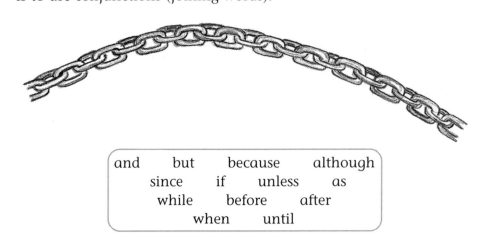

> and   but   because   although
>   since   if   unless   as
>   while   before   after
>   when   until

Here are two examples.

> You may not have noticed this, <u>but</u> first impressions are often entirely wrong.

In this example, the conjunction 'but' is placed between the two sentences.

> <u>When</u> the children woke up they found a list of instructions left for them by Count Olaf.

This time, the two sentences are joined by placing the conjunction 'when' at the start of the first sentence.

For practice (2)

Pick out the conjunctions used in each of the following sentences.

Remember:
* A conjunction may be either at the beginning of the sentence or in the middle

1 The children had to stay with Count Olaf because they had lost their parents.

2 When they met Count Olaf, the children took an instant dislike to him.

3 Although Count Olaf's house was quite large, the three children had to share one room.

4 The children felt very unhappy when Count Olaf came back home.

5 If the sun was shining brightly through the window, the children would wake up very early.

For practice (3)

Join the following pairs of short sentences into longer ones by putting one of the following conjunctions between the two sentences.

> although   but   while   because   when

1 The orphans tried to get used to the house. They could not.

2 The early morning sunlight disturbed the children. They were trying to sleep.

3 Violet made the curtains into a kind of cushion. The bed was very hard.

4 Klaus and Sunny soon became friends. They had not liked each other much at first.

5 Count Olaf left the children tasks to perform. He was out of the house.

For Further Study

More information and exercises on **Conjunctions and other methods of joining sentences** can be found in *Knowledge About Language*, pages 92–98

Chapter 7

Shoes were for Sunday (1)

Molly Weir was a Glasgow-born journalist and actress. The next two passages come from her autobiography, **Shoes were for Sunday**, in which she describes her childhood in the Springburn area of the city shortly after the First World War (1914–1918).

Rescue by tramcar

Up until 1962, public transport in the city of Glasgow was largely provided by trams which were powered from overhead wires and ran on tramlines laid in the middle of the roads. Here, Molly Weir remembers some incidents involving tramcars in her childhood.

1   One of the most dramatic stories told to me by my mother was of an accident to me in babyhood, when a tramcar was pressed into the rescue operation. I was about nine months old at the time and my mother had stood me up on the sink-ledge by the

5   window while she cleared up the bathing things before putting me to bed.

The china bath, washed and dried, was beside me on the draining board, and when I turned round at the sound of my father's key in the door, my foot went through one handle, and I

10 crashed to the floor. The bath broke into a dozen pieces, and an edge cut through the bridge of my nose like a knife. My mother used to shudder as she described the blood as 'spurting up like a well' but my father, quick as lightning, seized the two cut edges of my skin between his fingers, bade my mother throw a shawl

15 round me, and before she knew what was happening had dashed down two flights of stairs. He leaped on to the driver's platform of a passing tramcar.

'Don't stop till you get to the Royal Infirmary,' he ordered. The driver was so impressed with his urgency that he did exactly that,

20 and all the passengers were carried willy-nilly to the doors of the infirmary. To me the most impressive part of the story was that the tram wasn't even going near the infirmary on its route. It should have turned at right angles at the points long before then. I was astounded that a tramcar should have been used in this way

25 as an ambulance for me, and that the driver had dared vary the route from that marked on the destination board.

It was maybe this thrilling piece of Weir folklore which started my love affair with tramcars. When I was a little girl I only had the penny for the homeward tram journey, when my legs were

30 tired after the long walk into the town for special messages. It would have been impossibly extravagant to ride both ways. That luxury was only indulged in when travelling with Grannie, and the journey to town then seemed so different from the top deck of the tram, the landmarks so swiftly passed compared with my

35 usual walking pace.

When a halfpenny was laid on the tramlines it became a pretended penny after the tram had thundered over it and flattened it out most satisfactorily. To achieve this, we flirted under the wheels of the trams quite fearlessly, for we were so

40 familiar with the sight of them rocketing past our windows we saw little danger. I never knew any child to be injured by a tram. We were as surefooted as mountain deer, and the drivers were

> ### Extract continued
>
> quick to spot a faltering childish stumble on the rare occasion
> this happened, and to apply the brakes in good time. They'd all
> 45 played on the tramlines themselves when children, and our
> games didn't make them turn a hair. If a child was occasionally
> scooped up in the 'cow-catcher' – a metal shovel arrangement
> worked by the driver to remove any obstacle in his path – well,
> that was all right. Wasn't that what the cow-catcher was there
> 50 for? And it would be a good lesson for the youngster for the
> future.

Questions

Read lines 1–27.

1 In your own words, describe the accident that happened
to Molly when she was a baby.   *(2 marks)*

2 Name ONE of the things her father did to help her after
the accident.   *(1 mark)*

3 a) The writer uses a number of similes in the second
paragraph (lines 7–17).
QUOTE TWO of these.   *(2 marks)*

 b) Take ONE of the similes you quoted and explain why
you think it is a good comparison.   *(1 mark)*

4 QUOTE TWO verbs that show how quickly her father
moved.   *(2 marks)*

5 Why did Molly think it was unusual for the tram to take
her to the hospital?   *(1 mark)*

Read lines 27–35.

6 Which of the following best describes Molly's feelings about
tramcars, both as a child and as an adult?
 a) She found them interesting
 b) She was frightened of them
 c) She was fascinated by and admired them
 d) She was unsure of her feelings about them   *(1 mark)*

7 Give one piece of evidence that suggests Molly's family
was poor.   *(1 mark)*

8 Choose a word from the list to fit each of the
following meanings.

dramatic   folklore   extravagant
urgency   faltering   astounded

Meanings
a) stories from the past, handed down from one
    generation to the next
b) a feeling that something has to be done immediately
c) to act in a hesitant, unsure way
d) amazed
e) sudden, striking, full of action
f) wasteful with money   *(6 marks)*

Read lines 36–51.
  9 Why did the children place a halfpenny on the tram lines? *(1 mark)*

10 Which of these words best describes how the children felt
    when they were playing on the tramlines?
    a) confident
    b) nervous
    c) excited
    d) terrified   *(1 mark)*

11 Why were the tram drivers not too bothered when the
    children played on the tramlines?   *(1 mark)*

TOTAL MARKS: 20

Taking a closer look . . .

Genre

A genre is a type, or branch, of writing. For example, science-fiction,
fantasy, romance, history or travel.

Molly Weir's book belongs to the genre of **autobiography**.

An **autobiography** is when someone writes the story of his or her
own life.

A **biography** is when someone else writes the story of a person's
life.

For practice

The following titles were offered for sale in a recent mail order book
club catalogue. Match up the books with the genre of writing they
belong to. In some cases there will be more than one example per genre.

Feast by Nigella Lawson
The British Isles: A Natural History by Alan Titchmarsh
Himalaya by Michael Palin
Winnie the Witch by Valerie Thomas
Miss Marple's Final Cases by Agatha Christie
Football and all That by Norman Giller
The Lion, the Witch and the Wardrobe by C S Lewis
Forgotten Voices of the Second World War by Max Arthur
Treasure Island by R L Stevenson
The Hobbit by J R R Tolkien
Learning to Fly by Victoria Beckham (The star tells the story of her life in the Spice Girls and her relationship with husband David.)
Notes from a Small Island by Bill Bryson (An American journalist writes about his impressions of British life as he travels through the British Isles.)
The Fall of the House of Usher by Edgar Allan Poe (A grim story of a woman who is buried alive in the dungeon of a haunted house.)

Genre	Title
Crime	
Fantasy	
Sport	
Cookery	
Geography	
History	
Children's fiction	
Travel	
Adventure	
Horror	
Autobiography	

Chapter 8

Shoes were for Sunday (2)

'Entertaining Angels unaware'

In the second extract from her autobiography Shoes Were for Sunday, Molly Weir recalls her schooldays.

Extract

1   We always had Bible teaching first thing in the morning at school and one of the phrases which greatly puzzled me was 'entertaining angels unaware'. How could anybody be unaware of entertaining an angel, I thought? Surely they would be instantly
5   recognisable by their beautiful white wings and the clouds of glory round their heads? It never occurred to me that angelic qualities could be found in the most unlikely guises, hiding under very ordinary voices and in bustling everyday bodies.

My angel, as it turned out, hid inside the little figure of my
10   school-teacher, Miss McKenzie. To me she was always a little old lady, with her roly-poly plumpness, her slightly bowed legs, grey hair framing a round rosy face and caught up in an old-fashioned bun on top of her head.

She seemed so ancient that I was astounded to
15   hear her say one morning, in quiet explanation when she was a few minutes late, that she had been delayed waiting for the doctor to call to attend to her mother. Her mother! Surely she must be about a hundred!

20   Although I basked in Miss McKenzie's approval, I never really felt very close to her. We all held our teachers in some awe, and it never dawned on me to ask her advice as to what I should do when I left school. Surely there was only one thing to do? Get
25   a job and earn money to add to the household

purse as quickly as possible. But Miss McKenzie had other ideas. We in our house knew nothing of scholarships for fatherless children. The idea of a child from a working-class household going to college was the very stuff of story-books, and had

30 nothing to do with the business of living as we knew it.

Unknown to us, she bullied the headmaster into putting my name forward for a special scholarship open to children who showed some promise, and who would benefit from further education. As I was the school dux, he agreed, although he was a

35 bit worried about the expense of keeping me at college for a whole year from my mother's point of view. No earnings from me, and fares and clothes to be covered, for, of course, only the fees would be paid if I won.

Miss McKenzie brushed all argument aside. She came herself

40 with me to the interview with the scholarship board. To this day I can remember my utter astonishment when, on being asked if she felt I had any particular qualities, and would benefit from such a scholarship, this wee old-fashioned elderly teacher banged the desk with her clenched fist, sending the glasses rattling, and

45 declared in an American idiom I never suspected she knew, 'I'd stake my bottom dollar on this girl!'

I trembled at the passion in her voice, and at her faith in me. 'What if I fail her?' I gasped to myself. 'What if she has to pay all the money back if I let her down?' I knew we hadn't a spare

50 farthing to repay anybody, and I was sick with a sense of responsibility in case I ruined this new, violent Miss McKenzie. As I've said, I was a natural swot, but even if I hadn't been, the memory of that indomitable little figure would have spurred me on when I felt like faltering.

55 At the end of my year at college I was able to lay before her the college gold medal as the year's top student, a bronze medal as a special prize in another subject, twenty pounds in prize money, and a whole sheaf of certificates.

And suddenly as I gazed at her, and saw her eyes sparkling

60 with pride behind the gold-rimmed glasses, I realised how widely she had thrown open the door of opportunity for me. And I knew

> ## Extract continued
>
> for the first time what the phrase 'entertaining angels unaware' meant. For there, standing before me in class, was my very own angel, Miss McKenzie.

Questions

Read lines 1–13.

1 'Entertaining angels unaware'. (line 3)
Which of the following expressions do you think is closest in meaning to this?
   a) Thinking a person you know is better than he or she really is.
   b) Not realising how wonderful a person that you know is. *(1 mark)*

2 What did the writer think an angel looked like? *(2 marks)*

3 The writer, Molly Weir, describes her teacher, Miss McKenzie, as 'my angel' (line 9).
Pick what you think is the most likely reason from the following list:
   a) Miss McKenzie was very religious.
   b) Miss McKenzie was beautiful, like an angel.
   c) Miss McKenzie was especially kind to Molly. *(1 mark)*

4 Explain **in your own words** ONE feature of Miss McKenzie's appearance. *(1 mark)*

Reads lines 14–30.

5 Why was Molly so surprised when Miss McKenzie said she had been waiting for the doctor to call on her mother? *(1 mark)*

6 What did Molly expect to do when she left school? *(1 mark)*

7 What did Miss McKenzie think she should do? *(1 mark)*

Read lines 31–46.

8 QUOTE the word which shows that Miss McKenzie had some trouble in persuading the headmaster to support her plans for Molly's future. *(1 mark)*

9 QUOTE a sentence which shows how much faith Miss McKenzie had in Molly. *(1 mark)*

Read lines 47–58.

10 Find a word from this section of the passage to fit each of
the following meanings:

    a) strong feelings or emotions

    b) a feeling that it is your duty to do something

    c) stubborn, not giving up, not easily defeated   *(3 marks)*

11 **a)** What worried Molly most about going to college?   *(1 mark)*

    b) QUOTE two separate words or phrases that show
how worried she felt.   *(2 marks)*

Read lines 59–64.

12 'I realised how widely she had thrown open the door of
opportunity for me'

    a) Explain in your own words what this sentence means. *(1 mark)*

    b) Comment on the use of the word 'door' here.
[Hint: look back at page 11]   *(1 mark)*

13 We learn a lot about Molly Weir's character throughout
this passage. Write down ONE feature of her character.
Explain how you worked this out.
Lay out your answer like this:

Feature: _____   *(1 mark)*

Explanation: _____   *(1 mark)*

TOTAL MARKS: 20

Taking a closer look . . .

Writing in sentences (2)

a) We saw in chapter 6 that a sentence was a completed
statement. But sentences can take different forms. In the
previous extracts, Molly Weir uses at least four different types of
sentence:

Statement: The bath broke into a dozen pieces.
Command: Don't stop till you get to the Royal Infirmary.
Question: Wasn't that what the cow-catcher was there for?
Exclamation: I'd stake my bottom dollar on this girl!

For practice

Decide whether each of the following sentences is

    ★ a statement

    ★ a command

★ a question

★ an exclamation

1 Surely there was only one thing to do?

2 She was a little old lady with slightly bowed legs.

3 We in our house knew nothing of scholarships for fatherless children.

4 What if she has to pay all the money back?

5 He was a bit worried about the expense of keeping me at college for a whole year.

6 Come here this minute!

7 I went out to the cinema last night.

8 Give that back to her.

9 Are you feeling any better now?

10 She is the most incredible person I've ever met in my life!

b) Remember that every sentence should end with a full stop.

The writer of this extract has been very careless about punctuation. Rewrite it, adding five full stops.

> When Molly Weir was young the routes were indicated on the trams by colours later the colours were replaced by numbers people found it difficult to remember to look out for a number 25 tram when they'd been used to travelling in a red one it was easy to spot the colours a long way off but the numbers could only be read when the tram came closer sometimes this caused a delay at the tram stop if more than one arrived at the same time.

For Further Study

More information and exercises on **How sentences are made up** can be found in *Knowledge About Language*, pages 73–78

Chapter 9

On the Island

Iain Crichton Smith's book **On the Island** brings to life the pains and pleasures of a young boy growing up in a remote village near the seaside in the Western Isles of Scotland. In this extract two boys go out at Hallowe'en hoping to see a ghost . . .

Extract

1   "I'll tell you something," said Daial to Iain. "I believe in ghosts."

It was Hallowe'en night and they were sitting in Daial's house – which was a thatched one – eating apples and cracking nuts
5   which they had got earlier that evening from the people of the village. It was frosty outside and the night was very calm.

"I don't believe in ghosts," said Iain, munching an apple. "You've never seen a ghost, have you?"

"No," said Daial fiercely, "but I know people who have. My
10   father saw a ghost at the Corner. It was a woman in a white dress."

"I don't believe it," said Iain. 'It was more likely a piece of paper." And he laughed out loud. "It was more likely a newspaper. It was the local newspaper."

15   "Come on then," said Daial urgently, as if he had been angered by Iain's dismissive comments. "We can go and see now. It's eleven o'clock and if there are any ghosts you might see them now. I dare you."

"All right," said Iain, throwing the remains of the apple into
20   the fire. "Come on then."

And the two of them left the house, shutting the door carefully and noiselessly behind them and entering the calm night with its millions of stars. They could feel their shoes creaking among the frost, and there were little panes of ice on

25   the small pools of water on the road. Daial looked very determined, his chin thrust out as if his honour had been attacked. Iain liked Daial fairly well though Daial hardly read any books and was only interested in fishing and football. Now and again as he walked along he looked up at the sky

30   with its vast city of stars and felt almost dizzy because of its immensity.

     They were gradually leaving the village now, had in fact passed the last house, and Iain in spite of his earlier protestations was getting a little frightened, for he had heard

35   stories of ghosts at the Corner before. There was one about a sailor home from the Merchant Navy who was supposed to have seen a ghost and after he had rejoined his ship he had fallen from a mast to the deck and had died instantly. People in the village mostly believed in ghosts. They believed that some

40   people had the second sight and could see in advance the body of someone who was about to die though at that particular time he might be walking among them, looking perfectly healthy.

     Daial and Iain walked on through the ghostly whiteness of the

45   frost and it seemed to them that the night had turned much colder and also more threatening. There was no noise even of flowing water, for all the streams were locked in frost.

     "It's here they see the ghosts," said Daial in a whisper, his voice trembling a little, perhaps partly with the cold.

50   The whole earth was a frosty globe, creaking and spectral, and the shine from it was eerie and faint.

     "Can you hear anything?" said Daial who was keeping close to Iain.

     "No," said Iain. "I can't hear anything. There's nothing. We

55   should go back."

     "No," Daial replied, his teeth chattering. "W-w-e w-w-on't go back. We have to stay for a while. "

     "What would you do if you saw a ghost?" said Iain.

     "I would run," said Daial, "I would run like hell."

60   "I don't know what I would do," said Iain, and his words

Extract continued

seemed to echo through the silent night. "I might drop dead. Or I might . . ."

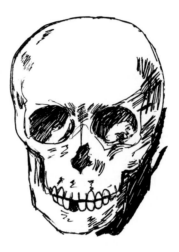

And then he stopped, for it seemed to him that Daial had turned all white in the frost, that his head and the rest of his
65 body were white, and his legs and shoes were also a shining white. Daial was coming towards him with his mouth open, and where there had been a head there was only a bony skull, its interstices filled with snow. Daial was walking towards him, his hands outstretched, and they were bony without any skin on
70 them. Daial was his enemy, he was a ghost who wished to destroy him, and that was why he had led him out to the Corner to the territory of the ghosts. Daial was not Daial at all, the real Daial was back in the house, and this was a ghost that had taken over Daial's body in order to entice Iain to the place where he was
75 now. Daial was a devil, a corpse.

And suddenly Iain began to run and Daial was running after him. Iain ran crazily with frantic speed but Daial was close on his heels. He was running after him and his white body was blazing with the frost and it seemed to Iain that he was stretching his
80 bony arms towards him. They raced along the cold white road which was so hard that their shoes left no prints on it, and Iain's heart was beating like a hammer, and then they were in the village among the ordinary lights and now they were at Daial's door.

85   "What happened," said Daial panting, leaning against the
door, his breath coming in huge gasps.

And Iain knew at that moment that this really was Daial,
whatever had happened to the other one, and that this one
would think of him as a coward for the rest of his life and tell his
90   pals how Iain had run away. And he was even more frightened
than he had been before, till he knew what he had to do.

"I saw it," he said.

"What?" said Daial, his eyes growing round with excitement.

95   "It was a coffin," said Iain. "I saw a funeral."

"A funeral?"

"I saw a funeral," said Iain, "and there were people in black
hats and black coats. You know?"

Daial nodded eagerly.

100   "And I saw them carrying a coffin," said Iain, "and it was all
yellow, and it was coming straight for you. You didn't see it. I
know you didn't see it. And I saw the coffin open and I saw the
face in the coffin."

"The face?" said Daial and his eyes were fixed on Iain's face,
105   and Iain could hardly hear what he was saying.

"And do you know whose face it was?"

"No," said Daial breathlessly. "Whose face was it? Tell me, tell
me."

"It was your face," said Iain in a high voice. 'It was your
110   face."

Daial paled.

"But it's all right," said Iain. "I saved you. If the coffin
doesn't touch you you're all right. I read that in a book. That's
why I ran. I knew that you would run after me. And you did.
115   And I saved you. For the coffin would have touched you if I
hadn't run."

"Gosh," said Daial, "that's something. You must have the
second sight. It almost touched me. Gosh. Wait till I tell the boys
tomorrow. You wait." And then as if it had just occurred to him
120   he said, "You believe in ghosts now, don't you?"

"Yes, I believe," said Iain.

"There you are then," said Daial. "Gosh. Are you sure if they don't touch you you're all right?"

"Cross my heart," said Iain.

Questions

Read lines 1–20.

1 a) What is Iain's attitude to ghosts?
   b) What is Daial's attitude to ghosts?   *(2 marks)*

2 QUOTE a line which explains why Daial has this opinion.   *(1 mark)*

3 The phrase 'Iain's dismissive comments' (line 16) means:
   (i) Iain did not take Daial seriously.
   (ii) Iain told Daial to go away.
   (iii) Iain agreed with what Daial said.   *(1 mark)*

4 What challenge does Daial offer Iain?   *(1 mark)*

5 Read lines 21–31.
   QUOTE two separate words or phrases which emphasise
   how quiet the night is.   *(2 marks)*

6 What do we learn about (a) Iain's interests and hobbies
   and (b) Daial's?   *(2 marks)*

7 'Now and again as he walked along he looked up at the
   sky with its vast city of stars and felt almost dizzy
   because of its immensity.' (lines 29–31)
   Which word in the sentence above is a metaphor?   *(1 mark)*

8 Re-read lines 32–35.
   How is Iain's attitude to ghosts changing?   *(1 mark)*

9 What did people in the village believe that those with
   second sight could do?   *(2 marks)*

10 What does Iain think he sees in lines 63–66?   *(2 marks)*

11 Re-read lines 70–84.
    a) Write out three separate words or phrases that make
        the story seem particularly frightening here.   *(3 marks)*
    b) QUOTE the simile which describes how frightened
        Iain was.   *(1 mark)*

Read lines 85–124.

> [In this section of the story, Iain tells Daial that he had a vision of a funeral – and that the body in the coffin was, in fact, Daial himself. Some people believed that if the coffin in the vision touched the living victim, that person would die. This is why Iain started to run, knowing that Daial would follow him. By doing this, Iain saved Daial from being touched by the coffin.]

12 QUOTE an expression which shows that Daial now has a greater respect for Iain than at the start of the story. *(1 mark)*

TOTAL MARKS: 20

Taking a closer look . . .

Direct Speech

Much of the passage about Daial and Ian takes the form of the actual words spoken by the characters. This is known as direct speech.

In a comic the actual spoken words might be put in a 'speech bubble':

However, when you are writing a story which includes conversations between people, follow these guidelines for the layout and punctuation of direct speech:

STEP 1: Speech marks

★ put the actual words spoken inside inverted commas (usually double inverted commas " ")

★ put a comma after the spoken words, but still *inside* the inverted commas. Add other words so that the reader knows who the speaker is (such as, *said Iain*)

★ then put a full stop.

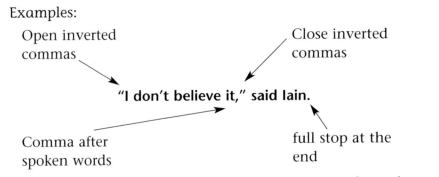

Examples:

Open inverted commas

Close inverted commas

"I don't believe it," said Iain.

Comma after spoken words

full stop at the end

Sometimes an exclamation mark or a question mark can be used instead of a comma after the spoken words. It depends on what the spoken words are.

"Did you see that film last night?" asked Amanda.

For practice (1)

Rewrite these sentences following the guidelines given above.

1 I'll tell you something said Daial to Iain

2 When are you going on your trip to Hong Kong asked Chris

3 I'm really looking forward to it exclaimed Tracy

4 I don't feel very well complained Craig

5 How about a bite to eat at Burger King suggested my friend

STEP 2: Who is speaking?

Almost every conversation consists of one person talking to another. To show when a new person starts speaking, you should start a new paragraph, like this:

"What would you do if you saw a ghost?" said Iain.

"I would run," said Daial.

"I don't know what I would do," said Iain.

Remember that you should never use inverted commas back to back like this

" . . ." " . . ."

Because you start a new paragraph for each new speaker, it is not necessary to say who is speaking each time, which can get monotonous.

"It was a coffin," said Iain. "I saw a funeral."

"A funeral?"

"I saw a funeral," said Iain, "and there were people in black hats and black coats."

It is clear that in line 1 it is Iain who says "I saw a funeral", since this is in the same line as his first words. Because we know he is talking to Daial, it is clear that it is Daial who says questioningly, "A funeral?", since these words are put in a new paragraph.

For Practice (2)

Write out the following piece of conversation, putting in inverted commas and starting a new paragraph for each new speaker. The first part is done for you to start you off.

"The big empty house by the station is supposed to be haunted," said Kirsty.

"I don't believe in ghosts," said Jennifer.

I'm not sure – my granny says she once saw a white lady and I don't think she would make it up, replied Kirsty. A white lady – what rubbish! Well, my granny says she saw it and I believe her, reported Kirsty. You'll not convince me, laughed Jennifer. If that's how you feel, I dare you to go to the station house – tonight! said Kirsty, furiously.

For practice (3)

To check that you understand the main rules for the use of direct speech, read the following sentences and select **one** of the answers in the brackets. You might underline the correct answer, or else copy out the sentence.

1   (*The actual words spoken / The verb of speaking and the name of the speaker*) are enclosed in inverted commas.

2   The punctuation mark at the end of the actual spoken words comes (*inside / outside*) the closing inverted commas.

3   When the actual words form a question (*a question mark / a comma*) is used before the verb of speaking and the name of the speaker.

4   When the actual words form an exclamation, (*an exclamation mark / a comma*) is used before the verb of speaking and the name of the speaker.

5   When the actual words form a statement, (*a full stop / a comma*) is used before the verb of speaking and the name of the speaker.

6   When there is a change of speaker, you should begin (*a new line / a new paragraph*).

7   If the same speaker continues after the verb of speaking and the name of the speaker, you should (*continue in the same line / start a new line*).

For practice (4)

Rewrite the following conversation, putting in inverted commas where necessary. Remember to start a new paragraph for each new speaker.

According to this newspaper report, Jack has been the most popular boys' name for the last eight years running, said Lewis.

I though it would have been John, said Emily.

It used to be, but John is now only number 62 on the list of the top hundred names.

What's the most popular girls' name? asked Emily.

It's Chloe, but I don't know any girls called that.

I do, said Emily. There are two in my class at school.

For Further Study

More information and exercises on **Direct Speech** can be found in *Knowledge About Language*, pages 106–108

Chapter 10

Paddy Clarke Ha Ha Ha

Paddy Clarke Ha Ha Ha by Roddy Doyle is about a ten-year-old Irish boy, Paddy Clarke, and his little brother who has the nickname 'Sinbad'. Paddy himself tells the story. Although the book is very funny, it also has a more serious side, since Paddy's parents split up and his 'Da' leaves home. The title of the book comes from the teasing words of his school-mates:

> 'Paddy Clarke
> Has no Da,
> Ha ha ha.'

Extract

1   Liam and Aidan had a dead mother. Missis O'Connell was her name.

    – It'd be brilliant, wouldn't it? I said.

    – Yeah, said Kevin. – Cool.

5   We were talking about having a dead ma.

    Liam and Aidan's house was darker than ours, the inside. That was because of the sun, not because it was scruffy dirty. It wasn't dirty, the way a lot of people said it was; it was just that all

10   the chairs and things were bursting and falling apart. Messing on the sofa was great because it was full of hollows, and nobody ever told us to get

15   off it. We got up on the arm, onto the back and jumped. Two of us would get onto the back and have a duel.

    I liked their house. It was

WINNER OF THE BOOKER PRIZE 1993

Roddy Doyle

paddy clarke ha ha ha

20 better for playing in. All the doors were open; there was nowhere
we couldn't go into. Once we were playing hide and seek and
Mister O'Connell came into the kitchen and opened the press[1]
beside the cooker and I was in there. He took out a bag of biscuits
and then he closed the door real quietly; he said nothing. Then

25 he opened the door again and whispered did I want a biscuit.

I liked sitting in the hollow of the sofa, just back away from
where the shape of the spring was. The material was great; it was
like the designs had been left alone and the rest of the material
had been cut with a little lawn mower. The designs, flowers, felt

30 like stiff grass or the back of my head after I got a haircut. The
material didn't have any colour but when the light was on you
could see that the flowers used to be coloured. We all sat in it
when we watched the television; there was loads of room and
brilliant fights. Mister O'Connell never told us to get out or stay

35 quiet.

The kitchen table was the same as ours but that was all. They
had all different chairs; ours were all the same, wood with a red
seat. Once when I called for Liam they were having their tea
when I knocked on the kitchen door. Mister O'Connell shouted

40 for me to come in. He was sitting at the side of the table, where
me and Sinbad sat, not the end where my da sat. Aidan was
sitting there. He got up and put on the kettle and he sat down
again where my ma always sat.

I didn't like that.

45   He made the breakfasts and dinners and everything, Mister O'Connell did. They had crisps every lunch; all I ever had was sandwiches. I hardly ever ate them. I put them in the shelf under my desk; banana, ham, cheese, jam. Sometimes I ate one of them but I shoved the rest under the desk. I knew when it

50   was getting too full in there when I saw the inkwell beginning to bob, being lifted by the pile of sandwiches underneath it. I waited till Henno had gone out – he was always going out; he said he knew what we got up to when his back was turned so not to try anything, and we kind of believed him – and I got

55   the bin from beside his desk and brought it down to my desk. I unloaded the packs of sandwiches. Everyone watched. Some of the sandwiches were in tinfoil, but the ones that weren't, that were just in plastic bags, they were brilliant, especially the ones near the back. Stuff was growing all over them, green and blue

60   and yellow. Kevin dared James O'Keefe to eat one of them but he wouldn't.

     I squeezed a tinfoil pack and it piled into one end and began to break through the foil. It was like in a film. Everyone wanted to look. Dermot Kelly fell off his desk and his head hit the seat.

65   I got the bin back up to Henno's desk before he started screaming.

     The bin was one of those straw ones, and it was full of old sandwiches. The smell of them crept through the room and got stronger and stronger, and it was only eleven o'clock in the

70   morning; three hours to go.

     Mister O'Connell made brilliant dinners. Chips and burgers; he didn't make them, he brought them home. All the way from town in the train, cos there was no chipper in Barrytown then.

     – God love them, said my ma when my da told her about the

75   smell of chips and vinegar that Mister O'Connell had brought with him onto the train.

     He made them mash. He shovelled out the middle of the mountain till it was like a volcano and then he dropped in a big lump of butter, and covered it up. He did that to every plate. He

80   made them rasher sandwiches. He gave them a can of Ambrosia

Extract continued

80 Creamed rice each and he let them eat it out of the can. They never got salad.

¹ cupboard

Questions

Read lines 1–5.

1 a) Write down the names of the two boys whose
   mother had died. *(1 mark)*

b) QUOTE ONE word from these lines which tells us
   what Paddy and Kevin think about this. *(1 mark)*

c) Explain what is surprising about their attitude. *(1 mark)*

Read lines 6–18.

2 Explain ONE thing Paddy noticed about the inside of the
   O'Connell boys' house. *(1 mark)*

Read lines 19 – 35.

3 a) Mr O'Connell was very strict with the boys. TRUE
   or FALSE? *(1 mark)*

b) Give a reason for your answer. *(1 mark)*

4 a) Give ONE reason why Paddy liked the O'Connells'
   sofa. *(1 mark)*

b) Name TWO things the boys did when they were on
   the sofa. *(2 marks)*

Read lines 36–43.

5 Name ONE thing about the O'Connells' kitchen that was
   the same as in Paddy's kitchen, and ONE thing that was
   different. *(2 marks)*

6 'I didn't like that.' (line 44)
   Explain ONE way in which this sentence stands out. *(1 mark)*

Read lines 45–65.

7 a) Paddy enjoyed the sandwiches he had for lunch.
   TRUE or FALSE? *(1 mark)*

b) Give a reason for your answer. *(1 mark)*

8 What TWO things did Paddy do when Henno, the
   teacher, went out of the room? *(2 marks)*

9 **a)** The other boys in the class were not interested in
       what Paddy was doing. TRUE or FALSE?   *(1 mark)*
    b) QUOTE one sentence in support of your answer.   *(1 mark)*

10 Read lines 70–81.
    Paddy describes Mr O'Connell's dinners as 'brilliant'.
    Give TWO reasons why Paddy thought the dinners
    were brilliant.   *(2 marks)*

TOTAL MARKS: 20

Taking a closer look . . .

Informal language

In his novel, *Paddy Clarke Ha Ha Ha*, Roddy Doyle tells the story
from the point-of-view of a ten-year-old Irish boy. He uses **informal**
language to present the thoughts and words of Paddy as this is how
a real boy would speak.

For Practice (1)

Find the **informal** expression used in the passage which matches
the formal expression given in column one. The first is done as an
example. The line number is given each time to help you.

Formal	Informal	
it would	_____it'd_____	(line 3)
mother	_____	(line 5)
dirty and badly kept	_____	(line 7)
getting up to mischief	_____	(line 12)
could not	_____	(line 20)
plenty of	_____	(line 33)
Sinbad and I	_____	(line 41)
father	_____	(line 41)
because	_____	(line 72)
chip shop	_____	(line 72)

For Practice (2)

Another feature of informal language is repetition. In formal
language, we try to avoid this.

One of Paddy's favourite words is 'brilliant'.

Can you suggest an alternative word or expression instead of 'brilliant' in the following sentences? Try to use a different one each time.

1 When we were on holiday in Spain the weather was **brilliant**.

2 *Gladiator* was a **brilliant** film.

3 My friend's Prada sandals are **brilliant**.

4 Mr O'Connell made **brilliant** dinners.

5 It would be **brilliant** to go to Mars in a rocket.

For Further Study

More information and exercises on **formal and informal expression** can be found in *Knowledge About Language,* pages 112–113

Chapter 11

The Wind Singer

The Wind Singer by William Nicholson is a fantasy novel.

Kestrel and Bowman Hath are twins who can read each other's minds. They set off on a quest which will enable them to find the 'wind singer', a device which will restore harmony and freedom to their country which is in the grip of a cruel dictatorship. After Kestrel gets into trouble with the authorities who have sent her to a special school, she and Bowman escape by jumping down a manhole into the sewers. Here, a new danger awaits them.

Extract

1   They made their way along the tunnel, up to their ankles in water, and slowly the light from the open shaft down which they had come faded into darkness. They walked steadily on, for what seemed like a very long time.

5   All at once the tunnel emerged into a long cave, through the middle of which ran a fast-flowing river. The light which faintly illuminated[1] the glistening cave walls came from a low wide hole at the far end, through which the river plunged out of sight. The tunnel water now drained away to join the river, and they found

10   themselves on a smooth bank of dry rock.

Almost at once, Bowman felt something terrible, very close by.

'We can't stop here,' he said. 'We must go, quickly.'

'Where are you?' said Kestrel. 'I can't see you.'

In answer, there came the hiss of a match being struck, and
then a bright arc of flame as a burning torch curved through the
air to land on the ground a few feet away from them. It lay there,
hissing and crackling, throwing out a circle of amber[2] light. Out
of the darkness stepped a small figure with white hair. He walked
with the slow steps of a little old man, but as he came closer to
the flickering light they saw that he was a boy of about their own
age: only his hair was completely white, and his skin was dry and
wrinkly. He stood there gazing steadily at them and then he
spoke.

It was the deep voice they had heard before, the voice of an
old man. The effect of this worn and husky voice coming from
the child's body was peculiarly frightening.

'The old children,' said Kestrel. 'The ones I saw before.'

'We were so looking forward to having you join our class,' said
the white-haired child. 'Follow me and I'll lead you back.'

'We're not going back,' said Kestrel.

'Not going back?' The soothing voice made her defiance sound
childish. 'Don't you understand? Without my help, you'll never
find the way out of here. You will die here.'

There was a sound of laughter in the darkness. The white-
haired child smiled.

'My friends find that amusing.' And into the pool of light, one
by one, stepped other children, some white-haired like himself,
some bald, all prematurely aged. At first it seemed there were only
a few, but more and more came shuffling out of the shadows, first
ten, then twenty, then thirty and more. Bowman stared at them,
and shivered.

'We're your little helpers,' said the white-haired child. And all
the old children laughed again, with the deep rumbling laughter
of grown-ups. 'You help us, and we'll help you. That's fair, isn't
it?'

He took a step closer, with little shuffling steps. As they came, they too reached out their hands. They didn't seem aggressive, so much as curious.

'My friends want to stroke you,' said their leader, his voice
50   sounding deep and soft and far away.

Bowman was so frightened that the only thought in his head was how to get away. He stepped back, out of reach of the fluttering arms. But behind him now was the river, flowing rapidly towards its underground hole. The old children shuffled
55   closer, and he felt a hand brush his arm. As it did so, an unfamiliar sensation swept through him: it was as if some of his strength had been sucked out of him, leaving him tired and sleepy.

Kess! He called silently, desperately. *Help me!*
60   'Get away from him!' cried Kestrel.

She stepped boldly forward and swung one arm at the white-haired child, meaning to knock him to the ground. But as her fist touched his body, the blow weakened, and she felt her arm go limp. She swung at him again, and she felt herself grow weaker
65   still. The air round her seemed to become thick and squashy, and sound grew far away, and blurred.

Bo! She called to him. *Something's happening to me.*

Bowman could see her falling to her knees, and could feel the overwhelming weariness that was taking possession of her body.
70   He knew he should go to her help, but he was frozen: immobilised[3] by terror.

Come away, Kess, he pleaded. *Come away.*

I can't.

He knew it, he could feel it. She was growing faint, as if
75   already the old children were carrying her away.

I can't move, Bo. Help me.

He watched them gather round her, but he was sick with fear, and he did nothing; and knowing he was doing nothing, he wept for shame.
80   Suddenly there came a crash and a splash, and something came charging out of the tunnel behind them. It roared like a wild animal, and struck out on all sides with wind-milling arms.

Extract continued

85

90

95

The old children jumped back in alarm. The whirlwind passed Bowman, pushing him off the bank and into the fast-moving river. Kestrel felt herself being dragged to the river's edge, and toppled into the water.

The cold water revived Kestrel, and she began to kick. Forcing herself to the surface, she gulped air. Then she saw the low roof of rock approaching, and ducked back down under water, and was sucked through the hole. A few moments of raging water, and suddenly she was flying through air and spray, and falling, falling with the streams of water, down and down, fighting for breath, thinking, this is the end, this is the smash, when all at once, with a plop and a long yielding hiss, she found she had landed in soft deep mud.

¹ illuminated: lit up
² amber: orange coloured
³ immobilised: unable to move

Questions

1 Read lines 1–4. ('They made … time'.)
Which TWO of the following made it hard for the children to walk along the tunnel?
  a) They were being dazzled by the light.
  b) The tunnel was ankle deep in water.
  c) There were jagged rocks in the tunnel.
  d) The floor of the tunnel was icy and slippery.
  e) It was dark in the tunnel. *(2 marks)*

2 Read lines 5–10. ('All at once … rock.')
Name ONE thing in the cave that was dangerous for the children. *(1 mark)*

3 The cave walls are described as 'glistening' (line 10). Does that mean they were wet or dry? *(1 mark)*

4 Read lines 17–22. ('Out of the darkness … wrinkly.')
Mention ONE thing about the child they met which made him seem like an old man. *(1 mark)*

5 Read lines 24–26. ('It was … frightening.')
   a) The child's voice was high and clear. TRUE or FALSE? *(1 mark)*
   b) Give a reason for your answer. *(1 mark)*

6 Read lines 31–33. ('Not going back? … You will die here.')
   Which ONE of the following words best describes the
   tone of the child's speech:
   helpful / threatening / friendly / impatient *(1 mark)*

7 What does the word 'shuffling' (line 39) tell us about the
   way the children were walking? *(1 mark)*

8 'They didn't seem aggressive as much as curious'. (line 47)
   Which ONE of the following sentences best explains the
   meaning of this:
   a) They were strange but they were really just trying to
      be friendly.
   b) They didn't seem hostile but they were interested
      in them.
   c) They were hostile and quite nosy. *(1 mark)*

9 Look at lines 53–58. ('The old children … *Help me.*')
   Pick out ONE adjective (describing word) from these lines
   that shows how Bowman feels after he has been touched
   by one of the old children. *(1 mark)*

10 Read lines 60–65.
   a) Pick out a single word which shows that Kestrel was
      not afraid to punch the white-haired child. *(1 mark)*
   b) Describe what happens to Kestrel's arm after she
      punches the white-haired child. *(1 mark)*

11 Read lines 67–78. ('Bowman could see her falling … wept
   for shame.')
   a) Explain in your own words why Bowman does
      nothing to help Kestrel. *(1 mark)*
   b) QUOTE a phrase which describes how Bowman feels
      at this point. *(1 mark)*

12 Read lines 79–85. ('Suddenly … toppled into the water.')
   This section tells of the children's friend, Mumpo, who has
   rushed to their aid.
   a) Pick out ONE word or expression which suggests how
      fast he came. *(1 mark)*
   b) Pick out ONE word or expression which suggests how
      noisy he was. *(1 mark)*

13 Look at the last paragraph (lines 86–94). Explain in your own words how it helped Kestrel when she was knocked into the water.   *(1 mark)*

Use information from the **whole** passage for the next question.

14 Which of the twins seems to you to be the braver of the two? Explain clearly ONE piece of evidence.   *(2 marks)*

TOTAL MARKS: 20

Taking a closer look (1) . . .

Onomatopoeia

This is a difficult word to remember, but it is easier if you split it into sections, and remember how it sounds, like this:

> ONO – MATO – POEI – A
>
> (like PEA)

Since this part of the story takes place in the dark, the sense of **sound** is important. The writer uses many words to express sounds.

Onomatopoeia is the figure of speech in which the sound of a word imitates the meaning.

For example, the word 'buzz' imitates the sound of a bee.

For Practice

The following sentences are all taken from the story. Underline (or write down) any word which sounds like its meaning.

1 It lay there, hissing and crackling, throwing out a circle of amber light.

2 At first it seemed there were only a few, but more and more came shuffling out of the shadows.

3 Suddenly there came a crash and a splash, and something came charging out of the tunnel behind them.

4 All at once, with a plop and a long yielding hiss, she found she had landed in soft deep mud.

Chapter 12

Ash Road

Ash Road by Ivan Southall, is set in Australia. At the beginning of the story three careless teenagers start a bush fire while they are camping.

Extract

1   It was early for Grandpa Tanner to be out of bed. He was up early because the heat was stifling, and the sun was already glaring, and the north-west wind that had blown all night was still searing[1] the leaves off the trees as it had seared them the day before.

5   Grandpa hated the north wind. He had hated it all his life. It was an evil wind, a wind that angered men and dismayed women and frightened small children. The long grass growing up to the house was as dry as straw, and dust was in the air, and the smell of smoke. It was the smell of smoke more than anything that had

10   got Grandpa out of bed and out of doors in his pyjamas.

   He could see no smoke in the sky, but it was in his nostrils, teasing them, and in his mind, in a way, prompting his memory back down the years to that one desperate hour when he had ⮞

15 faced an inferno[2] on his own and fought it on his own and beaten it on his own. He had prayed hard at the time, prayed for a wind-change, for rain, for an army of men with beaters; but none of these had come, and he had done it on his own, and had stood blackened and burnt and bare-headed in the paddock[3], in the prime of his strength, shaking his fist at the heavens.

20 An old bushman like Grandpa could smell eucalyptus[4] smoke on the wind from a fire burning fifteen or twenty miles away; he could smell it and feel it and see it with his eyes shut, with tingling senses, with an awareness that was electric. He stood almost motionless, every part of him tuned to that faint signal of
25 smoke.

Not in years had Grandpa seen real smoke – the savage, boiling, black-red smoke of a forest fire on the rampage. He had seen the smoke of scrub fires that had got a little out of hand for an hour or two; the smoke when farmers burnt off new ground, or
30 when shire-workers burnt off the roadsides; and the smoke when fire brigades were cleaning up hazardous pockets of bush before the full heat of summer (the boys of the fire brigades enjoyed a good blaze now and then). But he hadn't seen real smoke close to home since 1913. He had read of bad fires and seen far-off glows
35 in the sky by night, particularly in 1939, but those days seemed to have gone; there were too many people now.

Though the presence of fire always frightened him, Grandpa had never been unduly afraid of it. He knew that fires, unlike earthquakes or avalanches or erupting volcanoes, could be
40 stopped or turned. Men who knew what they were doing could even fight fire with fire. That was what Grandpa had done in 1913, and he had saved his farm though others not so far away had been wiped out. Even the township of Prescott had gone that day, 13th January. It had been there in the morning, and in the
45 afternoon it was a heap of charred rubbish and the Gibson family had been burnt to death.

That dreadful day had started like this one, even to the date of the month – the same searing northerly[5], the same faint smell of smoke, the same sort of temperature that had climbed and

┌───┐
│   **Extract continued**   │

50 climbed to over 112 degrees in the shade. And when the fire had
come over the top of the range and thundered into the valley like
a thousand locomotives[6] steaming abreast, it had become still
hotter and hotter – so hot that birds on the wing fell dead and
grass started burning almost of its own accord and locked up
55 houses exploded and creeks[7] boiled.
    But that had been a long time ago. It couldn't happen now.

[1] searing: burning
[2] inferno: huge fire
[3] paddock: field
[4] eucalyptus: gum tree
[5] northerly: north wind
[6] locomotives: steam engines
[7] creeks: streams

Questions

1 Read lines 1–10.
   a) Grandpa Tanner had got up at his usual time. TRUE
   or FALSE?   *(1 mark)*
   b) Give a reason for your answer.   *(1 mark)*

2 **a)** Grandpa Tanner was unusual since he hated the wind.
   TRUE or FALSE?   *(1 mark)*
   b) Give a reason for your answer.   *(1 mark)*

3 **a)** If a fire was started at this time it would burn easily.
   TRUE or FALSE?   *(1 mark)*
   b) QUOTE a simile from this paragraph in support of
   your answer.   *(1 mark)*

4 'He had faced an inferno on his own and fought it on his
   own and beaten it on his own.' (lines 14–15).
   Explain ONE way in which the writer's word choice has
   made this sentence effective and exciting.   *(1 mark)*

5 What figure of speech is used in the phrase 'blackened
   and burnt and bare-headed'? (lines 15–16)   *(1 mark)*

6 Read lines 20–25.
   Which of his senses did Grandpa Tanner mainly use to
   discover the fire: sight, touch or smell?   *(1 mark)*

7 Read lines 29–33.
   Explain in your own words ONE reason why fires were
   sometimes started deliberately.   *(1 mark)*

8 'Though the presence of fire always frightened him,
   Grandpa had never been unduly afraid of it.' (lines 37–41).
   Which of the following statements is closest to the
   meaning of this sentence:
   (i) Grandpa was very frightened of fire.
   (ii) Grandpa was not particularly afraid of fire.
   (iii) Grandpa was not at all afraid of fire.   *(1 mark)*

9 Read lines 38–40.
   Give an example of a disaster which, unlike fire, *cannot*
   be 'stopped or turned'.   *(1 mark)*

10 Read lines 40–46.
   a) Explain TWO things which happened in the great fire
          of 13th January, 1913.   *(2 marks)*
   b) Look carefully at the date of the fire. Why might
          some people think it was an unlucky day?   *(1 mark)*

11 Read lines 47–56.
   Explain TWO ways in which this day was just like the day
   of the great fire in 1913.   *(2 marks)*

12 'Like a thousand locomotives steaming abreast.'
   (lines 51–52)
   What figure of speech does the writer use here?   *(1 mark)*

13 In lines 53–55 the writer describes some of the amazing
   things which can happen in a bush fire. Explain ONE
   of them.   *(1 mark)*

14 'But that had been a long time ago. It couldn't happen
   now'. (line 56)
   These sentences are Grandpa's thoughts.
   Explain ONE way in which the writer has made these
   sentences stand out.   *(1 mark)*

TOTAL MARKS: 20

Taking a closer look (1) . . .

Personification

'It was an evil wind . . .' (lines 5–6)

A figure of speech used in this passage is **personification**, where a *thing* is treated as if it were *alive*. 'Evil' suggests that the wind has a nasty mind of its own.

For Practice (1)

Pick out a word from each of the following sentences which is also an example of **personification**.

1 The smoke was teasing Grandpa's nostrils.
2 The weeds had choked the flowers in the garden.
3 The sun smiled down on the warm sand.
4 The angry grey sky was a sign that a storm was coming.
5 The dry grass whispered in the light summer breeze.

Taking a closer look (2) . . .

Fact or Fiction?

Ash Road is a work of **fiction**. This means it was completely made up by the author. Ivan Southall has invented the **characters**, the people in the story, and the **setting**, the area where his story takes place.

Newspapers report facts. The following article was published in *The Scotsman* newspaper on Monday, 20th January, 2003. It tells of very similar events which really happened around that date in Canberra, the capital city of Australia.

The style of newspaper reporting is different from that of a novel like *Ash Road*.

For Practice

Read the newspaper article and then answer the questions. You could do this exercise in groups or pairs.

Four left dead as bush fires ravage[1] city

JOHN INNES

HUNDREDS of people in Canberra sifted through the charred[2] remains of their burnt-out homes today, after the worst bush fires in the history of the Australian capital left four dead and thousands homeless.

The raging fires forced mass evacuation[3] and destroyed at least 388 homes.

Hospitals treated about 240 people for burns and the effects of smoke from the fires that hit Canberra on Saturday. Many were residents who battled flames with garden hoses and buckets filled from swimming pools.

Fire crews said they were overwhelmed by the ferocity and magnitude of the flames. "I have been to a lot of bush-fire scenes in Australia . . . but this is by far the worst," said John Howard, the prime minister.

Police said a 61-year-old man died of smoke inhalation[4] while trying to save his house, and an 83-year-old woman died in her home. A 37-year-old woman was found dead at her bunt-out home, along with an unidentified body.

Officials said all fires had been contained[5], but some areas were still smouldering[6]. There were fears that strong winds forecast for Monday could re-ignite[7] the crisis.

Police patrolled charred and deserted neighbourhoods following isolated cases of looting and suspicions that some fires might have been lit deliberately.

At the height of the crisis on Saturday, when a state of emergency was called, fire-fighters called on people not to panic. Many residents reported no fire crews in their burning streets.

More than 20 per cent of the city was without power on Sunday morning and red-hot embers[8] fell, sparking fears that more lives and homes could be lost.

A mist of fine ash blew through the streets and a thick pall[9] of smoke hung over the city of about 320,000 people, which is surrounded by drought-hit farmland and tinder-dry forests. Strong, dry outback winds and soaring temperatures whipped up an inferno in its outer suburbs to the north, west and south, triggering unprecedented havoc on Saturday.

Mr Howard interrupted his summer holiday to tour the fire-scorched suburbs, where one resident told him of the speed of the fire.

"We just got a few precious things out and the family dog and within two minutes the house was just gone," Tony Walter told him.

---

[1] ravage: damage severely
[2] charred: burnt in places
[3] evacuation: moving people out
[4] inhalation: breathing in
[5] contained: kept within limits
[6] smouldering: glowing with flame
[7] re-ignite: set on fire again
[8] embers: pieces of burning material
[9] pall: blanket

Questions

1 Look at the headline.
   Write down TWO pieces of information contained in the headline.

2 Find TWO examples of real places which are mentioned in the article.

3 Write down TWO examples of statistics (numbers in figures) from the article.

4 Find ONE example of an interview. Write down the first few words and say who was interviewed.

5 Write down ONE example of a person's age being given.

6 Write down TWO phrases which make the story sound dramatic and exciting.

Checklist for newspaper articles:

- Writing is set out in columns
- A headline is used instead of a title, and sometimes sub-headings too
- Real people and places are mentioned
- Many statistics are given
- Numbers are written in figures
- Paragraphs are quite short
- There are few similes and metaphors
- Dramatic language may be used
- People have been interviewed and their exact words are quoted
- Peoples' ages are often given

Chapter 13

The War of the Worlds

There are plenty of books and films based on the idea of alien creatures coming to the earth from another planet. One of the earliest stories of this type was published in 1898 by H G Wells, a novelist who originally trained as a scientist. The story starts with a strange cylinder landing on the outskirts of London. It attracts a crowd of curious onlookers. Suddenly, the top begins to unscrew and a creature comes out . . .

1   I think everyone expected to see a man emerge – possibly something a little unlike us terrestrial[1] men, but in all essentials a man. I know I did. But, looking, I presently saw something stirring within the shadow – greyish billowy[2] movements, one

5   above another, and then two luminous discs like eyes. Then something resembling a little grey snake, about the thickness of a walking-stick, coiled up out of the writhing middle, and wriggled in the air towards me – and then another.

A sudden chill came over me. There was a loud shriek from a

10   woman behind. I half turned, keeping my eyes fixed upon the cylinder still, from which other tentacles were now projecting, and began pushing my way back from the edge of the pit. I saw astonishment giving place to horror on the faces of the people about me. I heard inarticulate[3] exclamations on all sides. There

15   was a general movement backward. I saw the shopman struggling still on the edge of the pit. I found myself alone, and saw the people on the other side of the pit running off. I looked again at the cylinder and ungovernable terror gripped me. I stood petrified and staring.

20   A big greyish, rounded bulk, the size, perhaps, of a bear, was rising slowly and painfully out of the cylinder. As it bulged up and caught the light, it glistened like wet leather. Two large dark-coloured eyes were regarding me steadfastly. It was rounded, and had, one might say, a face. There was a mouth under the

25   eyes, the brim of which quivered and panted, and dropped saliva. The body heaved and pulsated[4] convulsively. A kind of tentacle gripped the edge of the cylinder and another swayed in the air.

Those who have never seen a living Martian can scarcely

30   imagine the strange horror of their appearance. The peculiar V-shaped mouth with its pointed upper lip, the absence of eyebrow ridges, the absence of a chin beneath the wedge-like lower lip, the incessant[5] quivering of the mouth, the endless mass of tentacles, the deep breathing of the lungs in a strange atmosphere – above

35   all, the extraordinary intensity of the immense eyes – culminated in an effect similar to nausea. There was something fungus-like in   ➤

Extract continued

the oily brown skin. Even at this first encounter, this first glimpse, I was overcome with disgust and dread.

Suddenly the monster vanished. It had toppled over the brim of the cylinder and fallen into the pit, with a thud like the fall of
40 a great mass of leather. I heard it give a peculiar thick cry, and immediately another of these creatures appeared darkly in the deep shadow of the aperture[6].

At that my terror passed away. I turned and, running madly, made for the first group of trees, perhaps a hundred yards away;
45 but I ran slantingly and stumbling, for I could not avert[7] my face from these things.

There, among some young pine-trees and furze-bushes, I stopped, panting, and awaited further developments. The common[8] round the sand-pits was dotted with people, standing,
50 like myself, in a half-fascinated terror, staring at these creatures. And then, with a renewed horror, I saw a round, black object bobbing up and down on the edge of the pit. It was the head of the shopman who had fallen in, but showing as a little black object against the hot western sky. Now he got his shoulder and
55 knee up, and again he seemed to slip back until only his head was visible. Suddenly he vanished, and I could have fancied a faint shriek had reached me. I had a momentary impulse to go back and help him that my fears overruled.

[1] terrestrial: belonging to the Earth
[2] billowy: wavy
[3] inarticulate: unable to express yourself clearly in words
[4] pulsated: moved in and out regularly
[5] incessant: continuing without stopping
[6] aperture: opening
[7] avert: turn away
[8] common: area of open land

Questions

Read lines 1–8.
  1 When the cylinder opened, the bystanders expected to see:
      a) A human being
      b) An alien
      c) A creature resembling a man   *(1 mark)*

2 Which word in this paragraph means 'glowing in the dark'? *(1 mark)*

3 Read lines 9–19.
   Write down three individual words or short phrases
   which suggest a feeling of fear.   *(3 marks)*

4 Read lines 20–28.
   a) State one way in which the Martian creature
       resembled a human being.   *(1 mark)*
   b) State one way in which it did not resemble a human. *(1 mark)*

Read lines 29–37.
5 In this section of the passage the writer carefully selects
   descriptive words and comparisons to make the creature
   sound as unpleasant as possible.
   a) QUOTE one example.   *(1 mark)*
   b) Explain why you think this is an effective description. *(1 mark)*

6 a) Which feature of the Martian's appearance did he
       find most horrific?   *(1 mark)*
   b) QUOTE the words which make it clear that this is the
       worst feature as far as the writer is concerned.   *(1 mark)*

7 a) Which word in this paragraph means 'a feeling
       of sickness'?   *(1 mark)*
   b) Which word in this paragraph means 'reached
       a peak'?   *(1 mark)*

8 Read lines 38–42.
   The monster falls into the pit with a 'thud'. (line 39)
   a) What does this word tell you about the monster?   *(1 mark)*
   b) What figure of speech is the writer using here?   *(1 mark)*

Read lines 43 to the end.
9 What do you think happens to the shopman at the end
   of the passage?   *(1 mark)*

10 Pick out a phrase which shows how the narrator and the
    other spectators felt.   *(1 mark)*

11 Which word in the last paragraph means 'a sudden urge
    to do something'?   *(1 mark)*

12 Look back at the whole passage.
    What feature of the story did you find most exciting?
    Explain why. Lay out your answer like this:
    Feature _____
    Explanation _____ *(2 marks)*

                                                        TOTAL MARKS: 20

Strange but true . . .

RADIO LISTENERS IN PANIC

Many Flee Homes to Escape 'Gas Raid From Mars'

That headline actually appeared in a New York newspaper on 31 October 1938.

The night before, a radio dramatisation of H G Wells' *The War of the Worlds* had been broadcast, starring actor Orson Welles.

The setting of the story had been changed from London to New Jersey. The programme was so realistic that people thought the invasion was really happening! Hundreds of people fled from their homes to seek shelter elsewhere, and the police were swamped with phone calls from terrified members of the public.

Taking a Closer Look . . .

Fact or Opinion
For Practice

Read the two passages on the subject of UFOs (Unidentified Flying Objects) which follow. One is from an encyclopedia and the other is an eye-witness account of a sighting.

A) US Government investigations of Unidentified Flying Objects

In July 1947 a farmer called Mack Brazel found some unidentified debris scattered about his land near Roswell, New Mexico. The military authorities first stated that a 'flying disc' had been found but later said that the debris was in fact the remains of a crashed weather balloon. However, some people believed that the truth was being covered up for security reasons and there were even claims that the body of an alien had been discovered at the crash site.

The United States Government collected information on this and thousands of other cases, often keeping their findings secret. The object was to examine whether any of these unidentified flying objects were a security risk.

Various experts reckoned that 90 per cent of sightings could easily be explained away: some were simply stars, planets or meteors, while others turned out to be satellites or aircraft lights.

Now complete this table:

	True	False	Can't tell
1 In 1947 Mack Brazel found the remains of a flying saucer from outer space lying in his fields.			
2 The military authorities said that these remains had come from a crashed weather balloon.			
3 The body of an alien was found at the crash site.			
4 The American Government kept the public informed of their research into unidentified flying objects.			
5 A very small number of unidentified flying objects were flying saucers from outer space.			
6 The US Government investigated UFOs to discover whether they were a security risk.			

B) Eyewitness account of UFO sighting, Virginia, USA, 18th May 1955

I remember we'd been out walking the dog in the woods just behind the farm. I guess it would have been about half eleven at night. The sky was pretty clear and I remember Jim saying 'hey, look at how slow that plane's flying!' Well, I took a closer look and I said to Jim 'that ain't no plane!' I could see the thing quite clearly. It was completely circular and had a kind of silver rim right round it. At the front there were flashing green lights – about five or six, I think. We only saw it for a few seconds for it disappeared behind the trees. You know, I never really believed in UFOs before then but I sure do now! I don't care what anybody says – I know what I saw that night and I'll never forget it.

1 From the extract above, write down a sentence expressing a feeling or opinion.

2 From the extract above, write down a sentence stating a fact.

3 In your own words, explain TWO differences between the style of writing used in passage A compared to passage B.

> *Did you know . . . ?*
>
> ★ In 1997 100,000 people gathered in the town of Roswell, New Mexico, to celebrate the fiftieth anniversary of the Roswell International UFO Museum and Research Centre.
> ★ In the Museum there are displays of replicas of the aliens that eye-witnesses believed they saw in 1947.

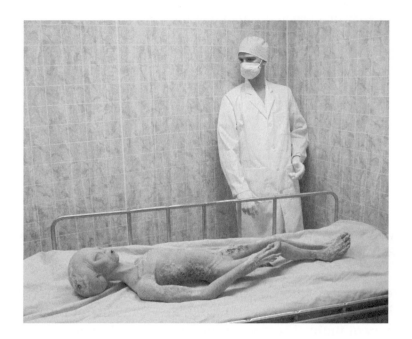

Chapter 14

The Lost Continent

Bill Bryson is an American writer whose best-selling books are very personal and amusing. Bill Bryson was brought up in a town called Des Moines, which is the capital of the state of Iowa in the Midwest of America, where life is old-fashioned in some ways. In this extract from **The Lost Continent** Bryson remembers the family holidays he had as a boy.

Extract

1   My father liked Iowa. He lived his whole life in the state, and is even now working his way through eternity there, in Glendale Cemetery in Des Moines. But every year he became seized with a quietly maniacal[1] urge to get out of the state and go on vacation[2].
5 Every summer, without a whole lot of notice, he would load the car to groaning, hurry us into it, take off to some distant point, return to get his wallet after having driven almost to the next state, and take off again for some distant point. Every year it was the same. Every year it was awful.
10   On vacations, my father was a man obsessed. His principal obsession was with trying to economise. He always took us to the crummiest hotels and motor lodges, and to the kind of roadside ➤

eating-houses where they only washed the dishes weekly. You always knew, with a sense of doom, that at some point before
15 finishing you were going to discover someone else's congealed[3] egg-yolk lurking somewhere on your plate or plugged between the tines of your fork. This, of course, meant cooties[4] and a long, painful death.

But even that was a relative treat. Usually we were forced to
20 picnic by the side of the road. My father had an instinct for picking bad picnic sites – on the apron[5] of a busy truck stop or in a little park that turned out to be in the heart of some seriously deprived ghetto[6], so that groups of children would come and stand silently by our table and watch us eating – and it always
25 became incredibly windy the moment we stopped, so that my mother spent the whole of lunchtime chasing paper plates over an area of about an acre.

In 1957 my father invested $19.98 in a portable gas stove that took an hour to assemble before each use and was so wildly
30 temperamental that we children were always ordered to stand well back when it was being lit. This always proved unnecessary, however, because the stove
35 would flicker to life only for a few seconds before puttering out, and my father would spend many hours turning it this way and that to keep it out of the
40 wind, simultaneously[7] addressing it in a low agitated tone normally associated with the chronically insane.

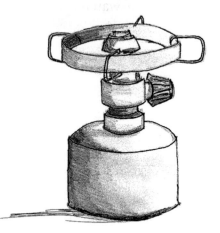

All the while my brother, sister and I would implore him to take us some place with air-conditioning, linen table-cloths and
45 ice-cubes clinking in glasses of clear water. 'Dad,' we would beg, 'you're a successful man. You make a good living. Take us to a Howard Johnson's'[8]. But he wouldn't have it. He was a child of the Depression[9] and where capital outlays were involved he

50 always wore the haunted look of a fugitive who had just heard bloodhounds in the distance.

Eventually, with the sun low in the sky, he would hand us hamburgers that were cold and raw and smelled of butane[10]. We would take one bite and refuse to eat any more. So my father would lose his temper and throw everything into the car and
55 drive us at high speed to some roadside diner. And afterwards, in a silent car filled with bitterness and unquenched basic needs, we would mistakenly turn off the main highway and get lost and end up in some no-hope hamlet[11] with a name like Draino, Indiana, or Tapwater, Missouri, and get a room in the only hotel
60 in town, the sort of rundown place where if you wanted to watch TV it meant you had to sit in the lobby and share a cracked leatherette sofa with an old man with big sweat circles under his arms. The old man would almost certainly have only one leg and probably one other truly arresting deficiency[12], like no nose or a
65 caved-in forehead, which meant that although you were sincerely intent on watching *Laramie*[13], you found your gaze being drawn, ineluctably[14] and sneakily, to the amazing eaten-away body sitting beside you. You couldn't help yourself. Occasionally the man would turn out to have no tongue, in which case he would try to
70 engage you in lively conversation. It was all most unsatisfying.

After a week or so of this kind of searing torment, we would fetch up at some blue and glinting sweep of lake or sea in a bowl of pine-clad mountains, a place full of swings and amusements and the gay shrieks of children splashing in water, and it would all almost be
75 worth it. Dad would become funny and warm and even once or twice might take us out to the sort of restaurant where you didn't have to watch your food being cooked and where the glass of water they served you wasn't autographed with lipstick. This was living.

[1] maniacal: crazy
[2] vacation: holiday
[3] congealed: hardened
[4] cooties: lice
[5] apron: tarmacked parking area
[6] ghetto: area where poor people live
[7] simultaneously: at the same time
[8] Howard Johnson's: chain of good restaurants
[9] Depression: time of poverty in the 1930s
[10] butane: bottled gas
[11] hamlet: village
[12] deficiency: lack of something
[13] *Laramie*: old TV Western series
[14] ineluctably: unavoidably

Questions

1 In lines 1–2, Bryson says his father is 'working his way
   through eternity' in Glendale Cemetery. Which of the
   following is closest in meaning to this?
   a) His father has a job in Glendale Cemetery.
   b) His father had died and was buried in
       Glendale Cemetery.
   c) His father likes to go walking in Glendale Cemetery.   *(1 mark)*

2 Explain ONE clue from the first paragraph (lines 1–9)
   which shows that Bryson's father was forgetful
   and disorganised.   *(1 mark)*

3 QUOTE an expression from the first paragraph (lines 1–9)
   which shows what Bryson felt about going on holiday.   *(1 mark)*

4 a) What is the meaning of 'economise' (line 11)?   *(1 mark)*
   b) Explain the information from the rest of the paragraph
       (lines 10–18) which helps you to understand the
       meaning of 'economise'.   *(1 mark)*

5 Which of the following is closest in meaning to the phrase
   'a relative treat' (line 19):
   i)   a very enjoyable occasion
   ii)   quite nice compared with some other things
   iii) something special to do with relatives.   *(1 mark)*

6 Read lines 19–26.
   Explain in your own words ONE of the problems that
   made the picnic places bad.   *(1 mark)*

7 Read lines 27–41.
   Tick the appropriate box against each of the following
   statements about the portable gas stove.   *(4 marks)*

	True	False
a) It was very expensive.	❒	❒
b) It took a long time to set it up.	❒	❒
c) It was perfectly safe.	❒	❒
d) It kept blowing out in the wind.	❒	❒

8 Read lines 43–46.
   What reason did the Bryson children give to their father
   that he should take them to a good restaurant?   *(1 mark)*

9 Which of the following is closest in meaning to the
   expression 'he was a child of the Depression' (lines 46–47):
   (i)   He was depressed because he didn't have much
            money.
   (ii) He had been depressed when he was young.
   (iii) He was young in the 1930s which was a time
            of poverty.   *(1 mark)*

10 Read lines 50–52.
   Give TWO reasons why the Bryson children did not like
   the hamburgers made on the gas stove.   *(2 marks)*

11 Read lines 52–54.
   Explain TWO things Bryson's father did when the
   children refused to eat the hamburgers.   *(2 marks)*

12 Bryson has invented the names 'Draino' and 'Tapwater'
   in lines 57–58.
   What impression do these names give of the places?   *(1 mark)*

13 Read the last paragraph (lines 70–77).
   Say whether each of the following statements is TRUE
   or FALSE:
   a) Bryson felt the difficult journey was worth it when
           they arrived at their destination.
   b) His father was always in a bad mood when
           they arrived.   *(2 marks)*

TOTAL MARKS: 20

Taking a closer look . . .

Hyperbole

Bill Bryson uses several techniques to make his writing humorous. One of the main ones is **hyperbole**, or **exaggeration**.

For example, in the first paragraph he says that his father would *always* forget his wallet, and have to go back for it 'after having driven almost to the next state.' Probably his father had just once or twice had to drive back a short distance to collect something he had forgotten.

For Practice (1)

Look at the following examples of hyperbole from the story. What do you think really happened in each case?

a) 'The kind of roadside eating-houses where they only washed the dishes weekly.' (lines 12–13)

b) 'A portable gas-stove that took an hour to assemble before each use.'(lines 28–29)

c) 'My mother spent the whole of lunch-time chasing paper plates over an area of about an acre.' (lines 25–26)

For Practice (2)

If you had to remind someone two or three times to return something they had borrowed, you might say angrily, 'I've asked you for it *millions of times.*'

Change the underlined expression in the following sentences to create an example of hyperbole:

a) This classroom is <u>very warm</u>.

b) The water in the swimming pool was <u>too cool to be comfortable</u>.

c) I <u>feel hungry</u>.

d) The bus stop is <u>not very near to</u> my house.

e) This bag <u>feels very heavy</u>.

Chapter 15

Bee Season

Bee Season by Myla Goldberg takes its title from a spelling competition called a 'spelling bee'. It is the story of an eleven-year-old American girl called Eliza who is in a bottom set at school and feels she is stupid compared to her clever brother, Aaron, and a disappointment to her father, Saul. She does not think she is popular, attractive or talented.

However, she discovers she is amazingly good at spelling. She is astonished when she wins a school spelling competition. After winning this, she goes forward as her school representative in a district competition and wins that also. She is now a finalist in the national competition.

Extract

1   When Eliza arrives home, Saul's first thought is how nice it is that the district bee gives away such huge consolation trophies. It takes him a few
5   moments of hearing his daughter's *"I won! I won!"* and feeling her arms wrapped around his waist to comprehend that the trophy is no consolation. He scoops his little girl
10 into his arms and tries to hold her above his head but realises, midway, that he hasn't tried to do this for at least five or six years. He puts her back down, silently resolving to start exercising.

"Elly, that's fantastic! I wish I could have been there. I bet it
15 was something else, huh, Aaron?"

Aaron smiles and nods, tries to think of what a good older brother would say. "She beat a lot of kids, Dad. You would have loved it."

"I know, I know. And I didn't even think to give you the
20 camera." Saul shakes his head. "But now I get another chance.
You're going on to the next level, right?"

Eliza nods. "The area finals are in a month. In Philadelphia."

Saul claps his hands. "Perfect! We'll all go. A family trip. A
month should give your mother enough time to clear the day. I'm
25 so proud of you, Elly. I knew it was just a matter of time until you
showed your stuff. A month. I can barely wait."

At which point Eliza realises that she has only four weeks in
which to study.

Studying has always been a chore on the level of dish-washing
30 and room-cleaning, approached with the same sense of
distraction and reluctance. The days following her spelling win,
she resolutely maintains her after-school schedule of television
reruns[1], pretends not to notice her father's raised eyebrows at the
sight of her in her regular chair, without a spelling list or
35 dictionary in sight. More than her father's unspoken expectations,
it is Eliza's growing suspicion that she has stumbled upon a skill
that convinces her to take out the word lists. She realises she has
never been naturally good enough at anything to want to get
better before. She renames studying "practice". Spelling is her
40 new instrument, the upcoming bee the concert for which she
must prepare her part. Eliza knows that something special is
going on. On Wednesday, she remembers the words she studied
on Monday and Tuesday. On Thursday, she remembers all the old
words, plus the new ones from the day before. The letters are
45 magnets, her brain a refrigerator door.

Eliza finally understands why people enjoy entering talent
shows or performing in recitals. She stops hating Betsy Hurley for
only doing double-Dutch jump rope at recess. If Eliza could, she
would spell all the time. She starts secretly spelling the longer
50 words from Ms Bergermeyer's droning class lessons and from the
nightly TV news broadcasts. When Eliza closes her eyes to spell,
the inside of her head becomes an ocean of consonants and
vowels, swirling and crashing in huge waves of letters until the
word she wants begins to rise to the surface. The word spins and

Extract continued

55 bounces. It pulls up new letters and throws back old ones, a fisherman sorting his catch until it is perfectly complete.

Eliza can sense herself changing. She has often felt that her outsides were too dull for her insides, that deep within her there was something better than what everyone else could see. Perhaps,

60 like the donkey in her favourite bedtime story, she has been turned into a stone. Perhaps, if she could only find a magic pebble, she could change. Walking home from school, Eliza has often looked for a pebble red and round, that might transform her from her unremarkable self. When Eliza finds this pebble in

65 her dreams, her name becomes the first the teacher memorises at the beginning of the school year. She becomes someone who gets called to come over during Red Rover, Red Rover, someone for whom a place in the lunch line is saved to guarantee a piece of chocolate cake. In the dream, Eliza goes to sleep with this magic

70 pebble under her head. The dream is so real that she wakes up reaching beneath her pillow. Her sense of loss doesn't fade no matter how many times she finds nothing there.

After a week of studying, Eliza begins sleeping with a word list under her head. In the morning it is always there, waiting.

¹ reruns : repeated programmes

Questions

1 Read paragraph one (lines 1–13).
   a) Eliza's father did not realise she had won the
       competition. TRUE or FALSE?   *(1 mark)*
   b) Give a reason for your answer.   *(1 mark)*

2 *'I won! I won!'* (lines 5–6)
   Explain ONE technique used by the writer here to show
   Eliza's excitement.   *(1 mark)*

3 'I didn't even think to give you the camera.' (lines 19–20).
   Which of the following reasons do you think is most likely
   for Saul not giving Aaron his camera to take to the
   competition?
   a) Saul did not want any more photographs of Eliza.

b) Saul did not expect Eliza to win.

c) Saul did not think Aaron would take a good photograph. *(1 mark)*

4 Read lines 20–26. ('"But now … barely wait."')
Saul is pleased that he will have another chance to see Eliza do well in a spelling competition.

   a) Name ONE *action* of Saul's which shows he is excited about this. *(1 mark)*

   b) QUOTE ONE thing which Saul *says* which shows he is very excited. *(1 mark)*

5 'Studying has always been a chore on the level of dish-washing and room-cleaning.' (lines 29–30).
Tick the box against the sentence which you think best matches this statement: *(1 mark)*

a) Eliza likes studying but does not like washing dishes and cleaning her room.	❐
b) Eliza finds studying just as boring as washing dishes and cleaning her room.	❐
c) Eliza enjoys washing dishes and cleaning but does not enjoy studying.	❐

6 Read lines 31–39. ('The days following … before.')
Say whether each of the following is TRUE or FALSE:

   a) Eliza gives up watching television in order to prepare for the spelling competition.

   b) Eliza begins studying because her father's 'raised eyebrows' shows he is upset.

   c) Eliza begins studying her spelling because she enjoys feeling she is really good at it. *(3 marks)*

7 'Spelling is her new instrument …' (lines 39–40)
Pick out ONE other word or expression in the rest of the sentence which continues the idea of spelling being like playing a musical instrument. *(1 mark)*

8 Eliza learns that it is fun to show off if you are very good at something. How did her school mate Betsy Hurley show off (line 47)? *(1 mark)*

9 Read lines 48–51. ('If Eliza could … news broadcasts.')

   a) Which word in this section tells us Mrs Bergermeyer is a very boring teacher? *(1 mark)*

   b) What does Eliza do to amuse herself during Mrs Bergermeyer's lessons? *(1 mark)*

10 Read lines 57–64. ('Eliza can sense ... self'.)
Eliza has a dream of finding a 'magic pebble' which will
change her into someone popular.
Pick out a word or phrase in this section which shows she
sees herself as nothing special. *(1 mark)*

11 Eliza thinks of several things that might happen if she
were magically to become popular.
Which THREE of the following does she imagine:
a) She will get a boyfriend.
b) The teacher will remember her name first in a
   new class.
c) She will get called on in the *Red Rover* game.
d) She will be asked to parties.
e) She will feel happy all the time.
f) Her friends will keep her a place in the lunch queue. *(3 marks)*

12 Eliza puts her word list under her pillow at night. Explain
clearly how her word list could change her life like the
'magic pebble' of her dreams. *(2 marks)*

TOTAL MARKS: 20

Taking a closer look (2) . . .

Spelling

For Practice (1)

The following list includes some of the words which Eliza had to
spell in order to pass into higher rounds of the competition.

Look at them for five minutes. Ask someone to read the list to you,
and see how many you get correct.

> tomorrow
> lizard
> weird
> secretary
> possibility

For Practice (2)

The letters of the following words have been scrambled. Can you work out how each word should be spelt? To help you know what the word is, an indication of the sound is given and there is also a definition of the word.

Cross out each letter in the scrambled word to check that you have included it.

Scrambled word	Sounds like	Means
teennces	sentins	a group of words
pesertaa	seperit	apart
freefindt	difrint	not the same
ceusinna	nyoosins	something annoying
lebutfiau	byootifil	lovely
snibusse	biznis	company

For Further Study

More information and exercises on **Spelling** can be found in *Knowledge About Language*, pages 46–57

Appendix: Further Revision and Practice

Word choice

Choosing one word instead of another can create a particular effect.

For example, consider the underlined words in these two sentences:

> Jim <u>plodded</u> along the road.
>
> Jim <u>walked</u> along the road.

In the first sentence, the word 'plodded' makes Jim sound tired or depressed, or as if he might be carrying a heavy load. It might make you feel sorry for him.

'Walked' is a more neutral word. We cannot tell much about Jim from it, and it does not arouse any special feelings in the reader.

For Practice a)

Say what special effect the underlined words have in the following sentences. A more neutral word is given in the sentence in brackets so that you can compare them.

1 Jenny <u>clung</u> to her mother's hand. (Jenny held her mother's hand.)
2 Billy <u>rushed</u> outside. (Billy ran outside.)
3 John <u>wolfed</u> his dinner. (John ate his dinner.)
4 The soldiers <u>trudged</u> back to their billets. (The soldiers returned to their billets.)
5 Steven <u>stole</u> into the office. (Steven went into the office.)

You might also think about whether a word is **simple** or **complex**. For example, 'house' is simple, while 'habitation' is complex. Sometimes a writer will aim to use simple words for a reason, such as to suggest the thoughts of a child. (See chapters 5 and 10, for example.)

Simple	Complex

For Practice b)

Make two columns headed like this.

Then write each of the words below in the appropriate column. The words are in pairs of similar meaning – one simple, another more complex.

elementary / easy   fun / entertainment   departed / left

delightful / nice   ascended / climbed   perceive / see

You could also consider whether a word is **formal** or **informal**. When deciding this, think of whether you would feel comfortable *saying* it. For example 'Mum' is informal, and 'mother' is formal. A writer may use informal words when he is aiming to give the impression that someone is speaking.

For Practice c)

Make two columns headed like this.

Formal	Informal

Then write each word in the appropriate column. The words are in pairs of similar meaning – one formal, the other informal.

terrifying / scary   Dad / father   disturbed / crazy

acquaintance / pal   brainy / intellectual

Word choice has many aspects, but the main thing to think about is what *effect* the word has on *you*.

Tip:

When you answer questions in a Close Reading test, you yourself should aim at using words which are **simple** and **formal**.

Figures of speech

Figures of speech are like decorations in language to make it more interesting.

The following five figures of speech are the commonest, and ones which you should learn to recognise.

The first three figures of speech all **compare** things. The things being compared will be alike in one obvious way, but unlike in others.

Simile: this comparison always uses the word 'like' or 'as'. For example:

The grains of sand sparkled <u>like diamonds</u>.
Clouds, <u>white as feathers</u>, drifted overhead.

Metaphor: this comparison does not use the word 'like' or 'as'. One thing is just said to *be* another. For example:

A <u>blizzard</u> of gulls followed the boat.

Personification: this is a kind of metaphor in which an object is spoken of as if it is alive. For example:

The car leapt forward with a roar.

These three figures of speech are known as **imagery**, and the things which are used in the comparisons (diamonds, feathers, blizzard etc.) are **images**.

Other figures of speech depend on the *sound* of the words.

Alliteration is the name given to the repetition of sounds at the beginning of words. For example:

'the forest's ferny floor'.

In this example the sound 'f' is very soft, like a whisper. It creates an impression of the quiet, still depths of the forest.

Onomatopoeia is an easy figure of speech to recognise, though not to spell! It is the name given to the technique where the sound of a word imitates the meaning.

For example, words like *sizzle*, *bubble* and *mew* all sound like their meanings.

For Practice

Say which figure of speech is underlined in each example. You could then discuss in groups or with your teacher why each example is effective.

1 The law's <u>as tricky as a ten-foot snake</u>.
2 Pike, three inches long, <u>perfect pike in all parts</u>.
3 The <u>hissing</u> geese were a terror.

4 The sea is <u>a hungry dog</u>.

5 Lights <u>blinked</u> along the runway.

6 Her hair was <u>a gleaming helmet of copper</u>.

7 The <u>whizz</u> of the Catherine wheel startled us.

Sentence structure

Sentence structure is the name given to the way words are arranged in sentences.

You might consider if the writer uses **questions** or **exclamations**.

Are the sentences short and abrupt or do they seem long and drawn out?

Is there any **repetition**?

Is there anything unusual about the **order** of the words in the sentence? The beginning and the end of the sentence are the **stress positions**, and words put there will be intended to stand out for some reason.

Does the writer make use of **direct speech**?

Does the writer tell the story himself, using 'I'? This is known as using the **first person**. Or does he write in the **third person**, using 'he', 'they' etc.?

Look carefully at the **punctuation marks**, and think about how they divide up the sentence.

Noticing techniques like these, and thinking about why they are used will help you understand the piece of writing more fully.

For Practice

Draw up your own checklist of things to look for in sentence structure questions. Make a list of bullet points.

Tone

When questions ask about 'tone', they want you to guess at the *feelings* the writer is aiming to put across.

For example, 'Let me! Let me!' could be described as an *eager* tone or an *enthusiastic* tone.

Look at the extracts of direct speech following, and then try to match them up with the tones given.

1 "Please don't leave! Please!"

2 "How dare you!"

3 "I wonder who the visitor can be? Do you know?"

4 "Well done! That is a really great achievement!"

5 "I can't see any point in going on with this. It will never be any good."

6 "Don't worry. I'm sure everything will turn out all right in the end."

7 "Keep going! You can do it!"

8 "What a shame!"

---

a) Pitying

b) Angry / offended

c) Depressed / disheartened

d) Encouraging

e) Congratulating

f) Consoling

g) Curious / inquiring

h) Pleading

This will give you an idea of what is looked for in a tone question. Of course writers can also express a mood in other ways, such as through descriptive details of setting, for example.

Answers

Authors' Note

The following pages contain suggested answers and marking schemes for the Close Reading tests and the language exercises in the 'Taking a Closer Look' sections.

The answers reflect what the authors had in mind while setting the questions, but they should not be regarded as prescriptive in all cases. It is very likely that other valid responses may be offered and teachers should use their own judgement in allocating marks for these.

Mary M. Firth and Andrew G. Ralston
2005

Answers

Chapter 1: The Kingdom by the Sea

1 The sound of the air raid siren woke Harry up. *(1 mark)*

2 Not scared *(1 mark)*

3 He had once tripped over a loose lace when dashing down to the air raid shelter. *(1 mark)*

4 Mark on merit: e.g., lights were not allowed during the black-out; a light might attract an enemy plane. *(1 mark)*

5 His (younger) sister *(1 mark)*

6 a) thundered *(1 mark)*

b) it emphasises how quickly and noisily he went down *(1 mark)*

7 hauling *(1 mark)*

8 roll of blankets / attaché case *(1 mark for each)*

9 'He'd done it all a hundred times before' *(1 mark)*

10 Because there was only one enemy plane and because it was still far out to sea. *(2 marks)*

11 Any two of: he deposited the equipment he was carrying on one of the bunks / located and lit the oil lamp / lit the candle / untied the bundle and spread out the blankets. *(2 marks)*

12 a) well-organised / thorough / knowledgeable / helpful could all be justified as choices. *(1 mark)*

b) any valid point: e.g. he knows the order in which to do things / he takes care over each task, etc. *(1 mark)*

13 a) they end in question marks *(1 mark)*

b) to reflect how uncertain / puzzled Harry felt *(1 mark)*

14 The bombs had fallen on or near the shelter / Harry had lost consciousness (*Not* that he had died, as the passage says he remembered saying 'seven'.) *(1 mark)*

TOTAL MARKS: 20

Similes

For Practice (2)

1 As bold as brass.

2 As cunning as a fox.

3 As cool as a cucumber.

4 Last night I slept like a log.

5 He ran like a hare.

6 She was as busy as a bee.

7 As quick as lightning.

8 He came down like a ton of bricks.

9 She was as light as a feather.

10 The baby was as quiet as a mouse.

For practice (3)

1 solution compared to key

2 snow compared to a blanket covering a bed

3 complicated network of streets compared to a maze

4 coldness of the stare compared to ice

5 education compared to a gate: both allow entrance to something

Chapter 2: Thimble Summer

1 'the hottest day'; 'one hundred and ten degrees Fahrenheit'. (*1 mark*)

2 **a)** simile (*1 mark*)

   b) 'like a bright skin'; 'as though a great hand beat upon the drum' (*either for 1 mark*)

3 There was no rain. (*1 mark*)

4 The oats were turning yellow (before their time); the corn leaves were dry and brittle. (*either for 1 mark*)

5 The mail is all bills which they have no money to pay. (*1 mark*)

6 setting the table (*1 mark*); fetching milk and butter from the cold room (*1 mark*).

7 Possible answers include 'still and dim'; 'peacefully'; 'coolness'. (*1 mark*)

8 **a)** 'charged' / 'lively' (*1 mark*)

   b) his hair was soaked with sweat / his face was red with the heat. (*1 mark*)

9 **a)** He is not happy. (*1 mark*)

   b) His words 'What a day' tell us he is depressed and has had a bad day. 'Shook his head' tells us he feels despair / unhappiness etc.; he looks tired, suggesting he is stressed. (*any one for 1 mark*)

10 **a)** quite far from (*1 mark*)

    b) it says that she had to go along a road, across a field and then over a large number of sand bars to get there. (*1 mark*)

11 Temperature / colour: it is warm and brown. (*either for 1 mark*)

12 She drops everything else she has found / she runs up to Jay to show it to him / she shouts happily /she calls it 'magic'. (*any two for 2 marks*)

13 **a)** FALSE (*1 mark*)

    b) He says 'magic!' in a sarcastic way; he says he doesn't believe in magic; he tells her not to be silly. (*any one for 1 mark*)

    TOTAL MARKS: 20

Describing Words

For Practice (1)

1 torn; brittle

2 big; black

3 dark; quiet

4 brownish; lukewarm

5 rich; muddy

6 small; glittering, silver

For Practice (2)

hot – hotter – hottest

bad – worse – worst

bright – brighter – brightest

tall – taller – tallest

lively – livelier – liveliest

good – better – best

cold – colder – coldest

cool – cooler – coolest

Adverbs

For Practice (3)

1 <u>Slowly</u> Garnet walked to the yellow house.

2 A spigot dripped <u>peacefully</u>.

3 Garnet <u>hastily</u> pushed the bills behind the calendar

4 The sun set <u>brilliantly</u> behind the trees.

5 Garnet ran <u>breathlessly</u> to show Jay the thimble.

6 "It's solid silver!" she shouted <u>triumphantly</u>.

Tone

1 angry

2 unhappy / depressed

3 happy / excited

Chapter 3: The Cay

1 In the middle of the night.   (*1 mark*)

2 **a)** simile   (*1 mark*)

   b) Alike : both move underwater / they are both deadly
   (*any one for 1 mark*)

   Unlike: sharks are living while submarines are machines / man-made.   (*any one for 1 mark*)

3 oil refinery on Aruba attacked / six lake tankers blown up.
   (*either for 1 mark*)

4 **a)** TRUE   (*1 mark*)

   b) FALSE   (*1 mark*)

   c) TRUE   (*1 mark*)

5 fresh vegetables / water / food in general   (*any two for 2 marks*)

6 **a)** an oil tanker   (*1 mark*)

   b) the oil and oil fumes could have caught fire and exploded (*1 mark*)

7 They came to see them off / they cheered / important people like the governor attended.
   (*any one for 1 mark*)

8 It was hit by a torpedo from the German submarine.   (*1 mark*)

9 **a)** Possible answers include sink / go down / disappear for ever.
   (*1 mark*)

   b) Mark on merit: It is an example of personification; It makes the ship seem like a living thing and so the reader is very moved at the sinking, as if by a human death.
   (*1 mark for simple comment showing awareness of personification, although not necessarily by name.*)

10 **i)** False

    ii) True

    iii) False

    iv) True   (*4 marks*)

TOTAL MARKS: 20

Nouns

For Practice (1)

Word	Yes	No
mother	✓	
send		✕
America	✓	
he		✕
after		✕
raft	✓	
cat	✓	
tiny		✕
fish	✓	
Timothy	✓	
eventually		✕
sight	✓	

For Practice (2)

common	proper	abstract	collective
shark house submarine boat pilot water	Aruba Montgomery	darkness victory destruction	crew

Chapter 4: A Dog so Small

1 The word 'piled' suggests how much mail there was for Ben. *(1 mark)*

2 A letter from his grandfather telling him when he would be getting his dog. *(1 mark)*

3 His grandfather had not given a firm promise / sometimes people break their promises. *(1 mark)*

4 **a)** angry *(1 mark)*

   b) he swept the parcel and packaging onto the floor *(1 mark)*

5 Any valid point, such as: his grandmother highly valued the picture / as it was given to her by Uncle Willy before he drowned / she was therefore showing her love for Ben by giving him something that meant so much to her *(1 mark)*

6 danger from traffic / lack of a garden or park to exercise the dog in. *(2 marks)*

7 Possible features might be: builds up his hopes that he'll get something he wants / childish – goes in a huff / bottles up his anger / finds it hard to express his feelings.
   (1 mark for feature, plus 1 for suitable explanation which illustrates that feature)

8 Keen to do something: eagerly/adverb *(1 mark each)*

An article valued because it is unusual or rare:
curio/noun *(1 mark each)*
A long journey, usually on board a ship:
voyage/noun *(1 mark each)*

9 **a)** false

   b) true

   c) can't tell

   d) true *(4 marks)*

   TOTAL MARKS: 20

Verbs

1. A verb is a doing word

For practice

(a) 1 expected; 2 pushed; 3 glanced; 4 brought; 5 said

(b) 1 sold; 2 read; 3 pushed; 4 picked; 5 assembled

2. Words like be and have are also verbs.

For Practice

1 He <u>is</u> a nice man.

2 My sister <u>has</u> a black cat.

3 We <u>were</u> on holiday last month.

4 You <u>are</u> on the list.

5 I <u>am</u> tired.

6 John <u>had</u> a new bag.

7 I <u>was</u> new at the school last year.

8 We <u>have</u> a black uniform.

9 My mother <u>is</u> a nurse.

10 You <u>have</u> a new hairstyle.

3. A verb can be made up of more than a single word.

For Practice

(a)

1 I <u>am going</u> to the party.

2 The team <u>has been trying</u> hard.

3 You <u>have seen</u> that film four times.

4 I <u>will be</u> on holiday nest week.

5 Partick Thistle <u>had beaten</u> Rangers.

b)

1 We <u>might be going</u> to America next summer, but my parents haven't made up their minds yet.

2 Barry <u>was being bullied</u> by John.

3 I <u>will be going</u> home soon.

4 The detectives <u>are looking</u> for the bank robber.

5 My sister <u>has been working</u> since 8 o'clock this morning.

4. Verbs can be in different tenses.

For practice

(a)

	Past	Present	Future
a) Ben's birthday <u>will be</u> on Saturday.			✓
b) Ben <u>hated</u> the picture.	✓		
c) My dad <u>paints</u> houses.		✓	
d) I <u>shall see</u> Jane tomorrow.			✓
e) A dog <u>ran</u> into the playground.	✓		

(b)

i) wake; remember; need; sit; rub; feels; are stuck; is; is; are.

ii) I woke up in a hot, dry wilderness. I remembered that we desperately needed water. I sat up and rubbed my grimy face with my hands and it felt like my eyelids and lips were stuck together. It was not far from dawn but there was none of the bright feel of sunrise in the air. The others were still fast asleep.

Chapter 5: When Hitler Stole Pink Rabbit

1 They were saying something about Anna / they were talking about something which affected Anna. *(1 mark)*

2 He thought the information might upset Anna. *(1 mark)*

3 a) Her brother, Max. *(1 mark)*

   b) She falls asleep before he comes to bed. *(1 mark)*

4 a) FALSE *(1 mark)*

   b) TRUE *(1 mark)*

5 Simile *(1 mark)*

6 a) her father *(1 mark)*

   b) A shower of coins fell on him *(1mark)*
   the coins completely buried him. *(1 mark)*

7 a) 'Sick with fear'. *(1 mark)*

   b) Her fear will turn out to be nothing but 'a silly night fear' / she will have a post-card from her parents. *(Any one for 1 mark)*

123

8 She had not had a post-card from her parents. (*1 mark*)

9 Mark on merit. Possible answers: 'terror'; 'came flooding back'; 'almost choked'; 'with such force'; 'Even though … she could still see it'. (*2 marks*)

10 It means that if anyone captures the person they will get a reward of money. (*1 mark*)

11 The family are going to move to Paris and their father is to fetch them. (*1 mark*)

12 b) She had not actually been very worried. (*1 mark*)

13 a) Write to Hitler and complain (since the amount of money was not very large) (*1 mark*)

   b) humorous (*1 mark*)

TOTAL MARKS: 20

Point of View

For Practice

At the end of the second week after Mama's and Papa's departure, my class went on an excursion into the mountains. We did not get back to the inn until evening. Then, although it was only seven o'clock, I went to bed. On my way upstairs I came upon Franz and Vreneli whispering together in the corridor. When they saw me they stopped.

'What were you saying?' I said. I had caught my father's name.

Symbolism
'A price on his head'

   a) Anna dreamed that a shower of coins fell on her father and crushed him.

   b) He would be killed.

   c) The coins which kill him in the dream symbolise the money which someone will get for handing him over to the Nazis who will probably murder him. Indirectly, money will cause his death, since he will be betrayed for it.

Chapter 6: A Series of Unfortunate Events

1 first impressions (*1 mark*)

2 a) they were very close to each other and got on well (*1 mark*)

   b) simile (*1 mark*)

3 a) a horrible person
   b) a depressing pigsty (*1 mark each*)

4 They tried to get used to living there OR tried to make things more comfortable for themselves. (*1 mark*)

5 Any two points such as: only one small bed / very dirty / had to sleep on the hard wooden floor / mattress on the bed was very uncomfortable (*2 marks*)

6 a) she used curtains to make a bed / tried to make a pillow for her sister (*2 marks*)

   b) she was considerate / unselfish / protective, etc. (*1 mark*)

7 To remind the children that Count Olaf was always watching them. (*1 mark*)

8 b) put up with (*1 mark*)

9 Explanation of one of the following: demanding / short-tempered / bad smelling (*1 mark*)

10 away from the house OR in the tower (*1 mark*)

11 repainting the porch / repairing
windows   (*2 marks*)

12 unsuitable   (*1 mark*)
the tasks required skills the children
would not have/they were too heavy
for children to do/they were too
dangerous for children or any other
valid reason   (*1 mark*)

13 any valid point if backed up with
appropriate evidence   (*1 mark*)

                    TOTAL MARKS: 20

Writing in sentences (1)

For practice (1)

Complete sentences:

1 Count Olaf's house was quite large.

2 Violet and Klaus took turns sleeping
on the bed.

4 The sun streamed through the
window.

5 Violet removed the curtains.

8 The house was a depressing pigsty.

Incomplete sentences:

3 Instead of toys, books or other things

6 If the people are interesting and kind

7 Your initial opinion on just about
anything

9 Without curtains over the cracked
glass

10 All over the house

For practice (2)

1 because **2** when **3** although **4** when
5 if

For practice (3)

1 The orphans tried to get used to the
house <u>but</u> they could not.

2 The early morning sunlight disturbed
the children <u>while</u> they were trying to
sleep.

3 Violet made the curtains into a kind
of cushion <u>because</u> the bed was very
hard.

4 Klaus and Sunny soon became friends
<u>although</u> they had not liked each
other much at first.

5 Count Olaf left the children tasks to
perform <u>when</u> he was out of the
house.

Chapter 7: Shoes were for Sunday (1)

1 *Sample answer:*
She caught her foot in the handle of
the china bath and fell to the floor.
The bath smashed to pieces and cut
her nose.   (*2 marks*)

2 Squeezed the edges of her nose to
stop the bleeding / carried her
downstairs and onto a passing
tramcar.   (*1 mark*)

3 a) Two of: Like a knife / like a well /
quick as lightning   (*2 marks*)

 b) Any valid point which brings out
the similarity between the two
parts of the simile.   (*1 mark*)

4 dashed / leaped   (*2 marks*)

5 The hospital was not on the tram's
route.   (*1 mark*)

6 c) She was fascinated by them and
admired them   (*1 mark*)

7 They could only afford to take the
tram in one direction.   (*1 mark*)

8 *Folklore*: stories from the past, handed
down from one generation to the
next

 Urgency: a feeling that something has
to be done immediately

Faltering: to act in a hesitant, unsure way

Astounded: amazed

Dramatic: sudden, striking, full of action

Extravagant: wasteful with money

(*6 marks*)

9 So that the weight of the tram passing over it would compress it and make it look like a penny.   (*1 mark*)

10 **a)** confident   (*1 mark*)

11 Because they used to do the same thing themselves when they were young/the 'cowcatcher' on the front would prevent injury.   (*1 mark*)

TOTAL MARKS: 20

Genre

Genre	Title
Crime	*Miss Marple's Final Cases* by Agatha Christie
Fantasy	*The Lion, the Witch and the Wardrobe* by C. S. Lewis
	The Hobbit by J R R Tolkien
Sport	*Football and all That* by Norman Giller
Cookery	*Feast* by Nigella Lawson
Geography	*The British Isles: A Natural History* by Alan Titchmarsh
History	*Forgotten Voices of the Second World War* by Max Arthur
Children's fiction	*Winnie the Witch* by Valerie Thomas (*The Lion, the Witch and the Wardrobe* and *The Hobbit* could also be included here)
Travel	*Notes from a Small Island* by Bill Bryson
	Himalaya by Michael Palin
Adventure	*Treasure Island* by R L Stevenson
Horror	*The Fall of the House of Usher* by Edgar Allan Poe
Autobiography	*Learning to Fly* by Victoria Beckham

Chapter 8: Shoes were for Sunday (2)

1 **b)** Not realising how wonderful a person that you know is. (*1 mark*)

2 They have beautiful white wings / clouds of glory round their heads   (*2 marks*)

3 **c)** Miss McKenzie was especially kind to Molly   (*1 mark*)

4 A paraphrase of any one of: roly-poly plumpness / slightly bowed legs / grey hair / round rosy face / hair caught up in a bun   (*1 mark*)

5 Molly could not believe that someone who seemed as old as Miss McKenzie had a mother who was still alive   (*1 mark*)

6 Start working as soon as she could in order to contribute to the cost of running the home.   (*1 mark*)

7 She should continue her education / go to college / gain qualifications   (*1 mark*)

8 Bullied   (*1mark*)

9 "I'd stake my bottom dollar on this girl."   (*1 mark*)

10 **a)** passion
    b) responsibility
    c) indomitable   (*1 mark for each*)

11 **a)** Any one of: letting Miss McKenzie down / not living up to her teacher's expectations / having to

pay back the scholarship money if she failed (*1 mark*)

b) Two of: trembled / gasped / sick with a sense of responsibility
(*2 marks*)

12 a) Miss McKenzie had given Molly chances in life she would not otherwise have had. (*1 mark*)

b) recognition of the fact that the word 'door' is used metaphorically
(*1 mark*)

13 Possible features might be:

- Molly was someone who paid attention at school / who thought carefully about what things mean (e.g. paragraph one)

- She created a good impression at school but did not confide in her teacher (paragraph four)

- She was willing to help at home (paragraph four)

- She was responsible / grateful (paragraph seven / nine)

- She was capable and hardworking (paragraph seven / eight)
(*1 mark for feature; 1 mark for appropriate explanation*)

TOTAL MARKS: 20

Writing in Sentences (2)

(a)

For Practice

Statement: 2, 3, 5, 7

Command: 6, 8

Question: 1, 4, 9

Exclamation: 10

(b)

When Molly Weir was young the routes were indicated on the trams by colours. Later the colours were replaced by numbers. People found it difficult to remember to look out for a number 25 tram when they'd been used to travelling in a red one. It was easy to spot the colours a long way off but the numbers could only be read when the tram came closer. Sometimes this caused a delay at the tram stop if more than one arrived at the same time.

Chapter 9: On the Island

1 a) Iain does not believe in them
(*1 mark*)

b) Daial does believe in them.
(*1 mark*)

2 'I know people who have [seen a ghost]' or 'My father saw a ghost at the corner.' (*1 mark*)

3 (i) Iain did not take Daial seriously.
(*1 mark*)

4 To go with him there and then to see if a ghost would appear. (*1 mark*)

5 'calm' / 'calm night'; 'they could feel their shoes creaking among the frost'
(*2 marks*)

6 a) Iain likes reading

b) Daial prefers fishing and football.
(*2 marks*)

7 city (*1 mark*)

8 Paraphrase of 'Iain in spite of his earlier protestations was getting a little frightened'. (*1 mark*)

9 They believed that people with second sight could foretell / predict that someone was going to die.
(2 marks)

10 Two of the following: Daial had become completely white / he had turned into a ghost / a skeleton.
(2 marks)

11 a) Possibilities include: 'he was a ghost who wished to destroy him' / 'Daial was a devil' / 'a corpse' / 'crazily' / 'frantic' / 'Daial was not Daial at all'.
(3 marks)

   b) 'Iain's heart was beating like a hammer'
(1 mark)

12 Possible answers: 'Gosh, that's something' / 'You must have the second sight' / 'Wait till I tell the boys tomorrow'.
(1 mark)

TOTAL MARKS: 20

Direct Speech

For Practice (1)

1 "I'll tell you something," said Daial to Iain.

2 "When are you going on your trip to Hong Kong?" asked Chris.

3 "I'm really looking forward to it!" exclaimed Tracy.

4 "I don't feel very well," complained Craig.

5 "How about a bite to eat at Burger King?" suggested my friend.

For Practice (2)

"The big empty house by the station is supposed to be haunted," said Kirsty.
"I don't believe in ghosts," said Jennifer.
"I'm not sure – my granny says she once saw a white lady and I don't think she would make it up," replied Kirsty.
"A white lady – what rubbish!"

"Well, my granny says she saw it and I believe her," retorted Kirsty.
"You'll not convince me," laughed Jennifer.
"If that's how you feel, I dare you to go to the station house – tonight!" said Kirsty, furiously.

For Practice (3)

1 The actual words spoken are enclosed in inverted commas.

2 The punctuation mark at the end of the actual spoken words comes inside the closing inverted commas.

3 When the actual words form a question a question mark is used before the verb of speaking and the name of the speaker.

4 When the actual words form an exclamation an exclamation mark is used before the verb of speaking and the name of the speaker.

5 When the actual words form a statement a comma is used before the verb of speaking and the name of the speaker.

6 When there is a change of speaker you should begin a new paragraph.

7 If the same speaker continues after the verb of speaking and the name of the speaker you should continue in the same line.

For Practice (4)

"According to this newspaper report, Jack has been the most popular boys' name for the last eight years running," said Lewis.

"I thought it would have been John," said Emily.

"It used to be, but John is now only number 62 on the list of the top hundred names."

"What's the most popular girls' name?" asked Emily.

"It's Chloe, but I don't know any girls called that."

"I do," said Emily. "There are two in my class at school."

Chapter 10: Paddy Clarke Ha Ha Ha

1 a) Liam; Aidan *(1 mark)*

b) 'brilliant'; 'cool'. *(either for 1 mark)*

c) You would expect them to think that the death of a mother would be a bad thing to happen to anyone. *(1 mark)*

2 It was darker / less sunny than their own / the furniture was falling apart. *(1 mark)*

3 a) FALSE *(1 mark)*

b) He does not get angry when he finds Paddy hiding in his cupboard. *(1 mark)*

4 a) He liked the upholstery fabric / it had plenty of room on it. *(either for 1 mark)*

b) Jumping off the back / having a duel on the back / sitting (to watch TV) / play fighting. *(any two for 2 marks)*

5 Similarity: kitchen table *(1 mark)*

Differences: O'Connells' had odd chairs; father's place was at the side, not at the head of the table. *(either point for 1 mark)*

6 It is in a paragraph by itself / it is very short. *(either for 1 mark)*

7 a) FALSE *(1 mark)*

b) He didn't often eat them / He says 'All I ever had' which suggests he didn't think much of them. *(either for 1 mark)*

8 He brought Henno's bin down to his own desk / He put all his mouldy sandwiches in the bin / He squeezed his mouldy sandwiches out of the tinfoil. *(Any two for 2 marks)*

9 a) FALSE *(1 mark)*

b) 'Everyone watched' / 'Everyone wanted to look.' *(either for 1 mark)*

10 He bought the food from a shop / he gave them chips and burgers which children like / he didn't make them eat healthy food like salad / he made mountains out of the mashed potatoes. *(any two for 2 marks)*

TOTAL MARKS: 20

Informal language

For Practice (1)

Formal	Informal	
it would	it'd	(line 3)
mother	ma	(line 5)
dirty and badly kept	scruffy/dirty	(line 7)
getting up to mischief	messing	(line 12)
could not	couldn't	(line 20)
plenty of	loads of	(line 33)
Sinbad and I	me and Sinbad	(line 41)
father	da	(line 41)
because	cos	(line 72)
chip shop	chipper	(line 72)

For Practice (2)
Possible answers:

1 excellent

2 wonderful

3 beautiful

4 delicious

5 exciting

Chapter 11: The Wind Singer

1 **b)** The tunnel was ankle deep in water. *(1 mark)*

  e) It was dark in the tunnel. *(1 mark)*

2 There was a fast-flowing river (which they might fall into and drown) / there was a hole in the floor which they might fall through.
(either one for 1 mark)

3 They were wet. *(1 mark)*

4 He had white hair / he had dry, wrinkled skin / he walked slowly like an old person. *(any one for 1 mark)*

5 **a)** FALSE *(1 mark)*

  b) Reference to or gloss of 'deep' or 'husky'. *(1 mark)*

6 threatening *(1 mark)*

7 They did not lift their feet / they dragged their feet along the ground.
(1 mark)

8 **b)** They didn't seem hostile but they were interested in them. *(1 mark)*

9 tired / sleepy *(either for 1 mark)*.

10 **a)** boldly *(1 mark)*

  b) Her arm becomes weak and floppy *(1 mark)*

11 **a)** He is very scared *(1 mark)*

  b) 'immobilised with terror ' OR 'sick with fear' *(1 mark)*

12 **a)** suddenly / charging / whirlwind *(any one for 1 mark)*

  b) 'crash'/ 'roared (like a wild animal)'. *(either for 1 mark)*

13 The coldness of the water revived her strength. *(1 mark)*

14 Kestrel is braver than Bowman. She is defiant: 'We're not going back', whereas Bowman 'shivered with fear'. In line 43, Bowman is so frightened

that he asks Kestrel for help, and she defends him bravely: 'Get away from him'. Bowman is too scared to help Kestrel as he is 'immobilised by fear'. He 'did nothing' to help because of his fear, and 'felt shame'. Bowman is described as feeling 'sick with fear'. Kestrel is not scared when she falls in the water but keeps going.

(Mark on merit: one piece of evidence to be clearly explained for 2 marks).

TOTAL MARKS: 20

Onomatopoeia

For Practice:

1 It lay there, <u>hissing</u> and <u>crackling</u>, throwing out a circle of amber light.

2 At first it seemed there were only a few, but more and more came <u>shuffling</u> out of the shadows.

3 Suddenly there came a <u>crash</u> and a <u>splash</u>, and something came charging out of the tunnel behind them.

4 All at once, with a <u>plop</u> and a long yielding <u>hiss</u>, she found she had landed in soft deep mud.

Chapter 12: Ash Road

1 a) FALSE *(1 mark)*

b) It says he was up especially early because of the heat / smell of smoke. *(1 mark)*

2 a) FALSE *(1 mark)*

b) It says men, women and children all disliked it *(1 mark)*

3 a) TRUE *(1 mark)*

b) The grass was 'as dry as straw.' *(1 mark)*

4 Mark on merit. Possible answers: repetition of 'on his own' to emphasize his isolation; list of verbs – 'faced', 'fought', 'beaten' – gives sense of action; repetition of 'and' emphasizes how much had to be done. *(Identification of one technique for 1 mark)*

5 Alliteration *(1 mark)*

6 smell *(1 mark)*

7 Farmers cleared ground / road workers tidied road verges / fire brigades cleared away fire hazards. *(any one for 1 mark)*

8 ii) Grandpa was not particularly afraid of fire. *(1 mark)*

9 earthquake / avalanche / erupting volcano *(any one for 1 mark)*

10 a) Grandpa saved his own farm; some farms were destroyed; the town of Prescott was destroyed; the Gibson family were burnt to death. *(any two for 2 marks)*

b) The date was the 13th; the number 13 is often considered unlucky. *(1 mark)*

11 Same date / a north wind was blowing / the smell of smoke / it was very hot. *(any two for 2 marks)*

12 simile *(1 mark)*

13 birds dropped dead while flying / grass started burning spontaneously / houses were exploding / small rivers were boiling. *(any one for 1 mark)*

14 They are in a paragraph by themselves / they are short / the tone is very definite, confident although he is wrong / they are ironic since it is happening now. *(any one for 1 mark)*

TOTAL MARKS: 20

Personification

For Practice (1)

1 The smoke was <u>teasing</u> Grandpa's nostrils.
2 The weeds had <u>choked</u> the flowers in the garden.
3 The sun <u>smiled</u> down on the warm sand.
4 The <u>angry</u> grey sky was a sign that a storm was coming.
5 The dry grass <u>whispered</u> in the light summer breeze.

Fact or Fiction

1 Four people have died in the fire; there are major fires raging across the countryside; a city has had a lot of damage.
2 Canberra; Australia
3 20% of the city has no power; 388 homes have been destroyed; 240 people were treated for burns and smoke inhalation; the city has 20,000 inhabitants.
4 John Howard, the Prime Minister: 'I have been ...'
   Tony Walter, a victim of the fire: 'We just got a few ...'
5 A 61 year old man; an 83 year old woman; a 37 year old woman.
6 'raging fires'; 'battled flames'; 'whipped up an inferno'.

Chapter 13: The War of the Worlds

1 **c)** A creature resembling a man (*1 mark*)
2 luminous (*1 mark*)
3 Any three of the following: sudden chill / loud shriek / horror / inarticulate exclamations / ungovernable terror / petrified and staring (*3 marks*)
4 **a)** One of the following: eyes / face / mouth / saliva (*1 mark*)
   b) One of the following: larger in size / colour – greyish / texture like leather / mouth was under its eyes / it had tentacles. (*1 mark*)
5 **a)** Possible examples include 'incessant quivering of the mouth'; 'fungus-like; 'oily brown skin' (*1 mark*)
   b) Mark on merit, as appropriate to example. (*1 mark*)
6 **a)** the huge eyes (*1 mark*)
   b) above all (*1 mark*)
7 **a)** nausea (*1 mark*)
   b) culminated (*1 mark*)
8 **a)** It was very heavy (*1 mark*)
   b) onomatopoeia (*1 mark*)
9 He is probably killed by the creature. (*1 mark*)
10 'half-fascinated terror' (*1 mark*)
11 impulse (*1 mark*)
12 Mark on merit – one mark for identifying a feature; one mark for relevant explanation. (*2 marks*)

TOTAL MARKS: 20

Fact or Opinion

For Practice

(a)
1 False
2 True
3 False
4 False
5 Can't tell
6 True

For Practice

(b)

1 'I never really believed in UFOs before then but I sure do now.'

2 'The sky was pretty clear.'

3 *Differences:* Passage A is impersonal, factual, precise (dates, statistics, etc.).

Passage B is personal. It includes more description and emphasises feelings and involvement.

Chapter 14: The Lost Continent

1 b) His father had died and was buried in Glendale Cemetery.
(1 mark)

2 His father did not give them much warning about the holiday, but took off very suddenly / he often forgot something like his wallet and had to go back for it. *(either one for 1 mark)*

3 '(It was) awful' *(1 mark)*

4 a) save money / spend as little as possible. *(1 mark)*

b) He went to cheap and nasty hotels and restaurants. *(1 mark)*

5 ii) quite nice compared with some other things *(1 mark)*

6 It would be near a parking area for lorries and trucks / it would be in a poor and rough area and children would pester them for food / it would get very windy *(any one for 1 mark)*

7 a) FALSE

b) TRUE

c) FALSE

d) TRUE *(4 marks)*

8 He had a good job and he could afford it. *(1 mark)*

9 (iii) He was young in the 1930s which was a time of poverty.
(1 mark)

10 They were cold / uncooked / smelled of fuel (Butane) *(any two for 2 marks)*

11 He became angry / lost his temper *(1 mark)*

and took them to a restaurant / diner *(1 mark)*

12 They sound dull / dirty. *(1 mark)*

13 a) TRUE *(1 mark)*

b) FALSE *(1 mark)*

TOTAL MARKS: 20

Hyperbole

For Practice (1)

a) The dishes were not always perfectly clean.

b) The stove was complicated and took quite a long time to set up.

c) His mother would sometimes have to pick up paper plates which had blown off the picnic table.

For Practice (2)

Possibilities include:

a) This classroom is boiling.

b) The water in the swimming pool was freezing.

c) I am starving.

d) The bus stop is miles from my house.

e) This bag weighs a ton.

Chapter 15: Bee Season

1 **a)** TRUE *(1 mark)*

   b) He thinks her cup is just a consolation prize for losers / it takes him quite a while of listening to her saying 'I won' to understand. *(either one for 1 mark)*

2 Repetition / italics / exclamation marks. *(any one for 1 mark)*

3 **b)** Saul did not expect Eliza to win. *(1 mark)*

4 **a)** He claps *(1 mark)*

   b) Possible answers include 'Perfect' / 'We'll all go' / 'I can barely wait'. *(1 mark)*

5 **b)** Eliza finds studying just as boring as washing dishes and cleaning her room. *(1 mark)*

6 **a)** FALSE *(1 mark)*

   b) FALSE *(1 mark)*

   c) TRUE *(1 mark)*

7 concert / (prepare her) part *(either for 1 mark)*

8 using a skipping / jumping rope *(1 mark)*

9 **a)** droning *(1 mark)*

   b) She starts thinking of how the words Mrs Bergermeyer uses are spelt. *(1 mark)*

10 unremarkable / her unremarkable self *(1 mark)*

11 **b)** The teacher will remember her name first in a new class. *(1 mark)*

   c) She will get called on in the *Red Rover* game. *(1 mark)*

   f) Her friends will keep her a place in the lunch queue *(1 mark)*

12 Mark on merit: e.g., she could gain confidence through winning the spelling competition.
(2 marks for clear explanation)
TOTAL MARKS: 20

Spelling
Scrambled words:

   sentence

   separate

   different

   nuisance

   beautiful

   business

Appendix: Further Revision and Practice

Word Choice

1 'Clung' suggests Jenny felt desperate and afraid and held on very tightly as if she would never let go.

2 'Rushed' suggests he ran out at high speed and with great urgency.

3 'Wolfed' suggests eating very fast and hungrily, without attention to table manners.

4 'Trudged' suggests the soldiers were tired or in low spirits – it suggests a heavy tread.

5 'Stole' suggests he went furtively, trying not to be observed.

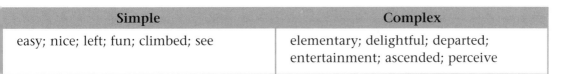

Simple	Complex
easy; nice; left; fun; climbed; see	elementary; delightful; departed; entertainment; ascended; perceive

Formal	Informal
terrifying; acquaintance; disturbed; father; intellectual	scary; pal; crazy; Dad; brainy

Figures of Speech

1 simile
2 alliteration
3 onomatopoeia
4 metaphor
5 personification
6 metaphor
7 onomatopoeia

Tone

1 **(h)** pleading
2 **(b)** angry / offended
3 **(g)** curious / inquiring
4 **(e)** congratulating
5 **(c)** depressed / disheartened
6 **(f)** consoling
7 **(d)** encouraging
8 **(a)** pitying